Chapel Lock Hospital.

The Collection of Psalm and Hymn Tunes,

Sung at the Chapel of the Lock Hospital

Chapel Lock Hospital.

The Collection of Psalm and Hymn Tunes,
Sung at the Chapel of the Lock Hospital

ISBN/EAN: 9783744784986

Printed in Europe, USA, Canada, Australia, Japan

Cover: Foto ©Thomas Meinert / pixelio.de

More available books at **www.hansebooks.com**

A New

AND

IMPROVED EDITION OF

The Collection of

PSALM & HYMN TUNES,

sung at the CHAPEL of the LOCK HOSPITAL

Book 1. 2. 3. & 4.   Price 20.

London

Printed by Broderip & Wilkinson, 13 Hay-market

Where are Printed, the 1.st 2.nd 3.rd & 4.th Books of the Magdalen Hymns. 2.s each

INDEX
Nº I.

The Second Advent.

Set by M.M.

He comes! He comes, the Judge severe! The seventh Trumpet

He comes! He comes, the Judge severe! The seventh Trumpet

speaks him near! His Lightnings flash, his Thunders roll, He's

speaks him near! His Lightnings flash, his Thunders roll, He's

welcome to the faithful Soul, Wel-come wel-come

welcome to the faithful Soul, Wel-come wel-come

welcome, welcome, welcome to the faithful Soul.

welcome, welcome, welcome to the faithful Soul.

2

From Heav'n angelic Voices sound,
See the Almighty Jesus crown'd;
Girt with Omnipotence and Grace,
And Glory decks the Saviour's Face.
Glory, Glory, Glory, Glory, Glory decks the Saviour's Face.

3

Descending on his Azure Throne,
He claims the Kingdoms for his own;
The Kingdoms all obey his Word,
And hail him their triumphant Lord.
Hail him, hail him, hail him, hail him, hail him their
triumphant Lord.

4

Shout all the People of the Sky,
And all the Saints of the Most High;
Our God, who now his Right obtains,
For ever and for ever Reigns;
Ever, ever, ever, ever, ever and for ever Reigns.

5

The Father praise, the Son adore,
The Spirit bless for evermore;
Salvation's glorious Work is done,
We welcome Thee Great Three in One!
Welcome, welcome, welcome, welcome, welcome Thee
Great Three in One.

Patient's Tune

Set by F.G.

Ye Servants of God whose diligent Care,

Ye Servants of God whose diligent Care,

Is ever employ'd in Watching and Pray'r

Is ever employ'd in Watching and Pray'r

With Praises unceasing Your Jesus proclaim,

With Praises unceasing Your Jesus proclaim,

Re .. joicing and blessing His ex - cel - lent Name.

Re .. joicing and blessing His ex - cel - lent Name.

Re .. joi.cing and blefsing his ex . cel . lent Name.

Re .. joi.cing and blefsing his ex . cel . lent Name.

(2)

'Tis Jesus commands, Come all to his House,
And lift up your Hands, And pay him your Vows;
And whilst ye are giving Your Jesus his Due,
The Lord out of Heaven Shall sanctify you .

Lock Tune

Set by H. B.

Ye Servants of God, Your Master pro-claim,

Ye Servants of God, Your Master pro-claim,

And publish a--broad His won-der-ful Name.

And publish a--broad His won-der-ful Name.

The Name all-vic-to-ri-ous of Je-sus ex--tol

The Name all-vic-to-ri-ous of Je-sus ex--tol

His Kingdom is Glorious and rules o--ver all.

His Kingdom is Glorious and rules o--ver all.

2

God ruleth on high,
    Almighty to save,
And still he is nigh,
    His Presence we have,
The great Congregation
    His Triumph shall sing,
Ascribing Salvation
    To Jesus our King.

3

Salvation to God,
    Who sits on the Throne,
Let all cry aloud,
    And honour the Son:
Our Jesus's Praises
    The Angels proclaim,
Fall down on their Faces,
    And worship the Lamb.

4

Then let us adore
    And give him his Right,
All Glory and Pow'r,
    And Wisdom, and Might;
All Honour and Blessing,
    With Angels above,
And Thanks never ceasing,
    And infinite Love.

Blendon

Jesus my all to Heav'n is gone, He whom I fix my Hopes up - - - on; His Track I see and I'll pur - - sue the nar - row Way, 'till Him I view.

2

The Way the holy Prophets went,
The Road that leads from Banishment,
The King's Highway of Holiness,
I'll go, for all his Paths are Peace.

3

No Stranger may proceed therein,
No Lover of the World and Sin,
No Lion, no devouring Care,
No Sin, nor Sorrow shall be there.

4

No, nothing may go up thereon,
But trav'ling Souls, and I am one;
Way-faring Men, to Cannaan bound,
Shall only in the Way be found.

5

This is the Way I long have sought,
And mourn'd because I found it not;
My Grief a Burden long has been,
Because I cou'd not cease from Sin.

6

The more I strove against it's Pow'r,
I sinn'd and stumbled but the more,
Till late I heard my Saviour say
"Come hither, Soul. I am the Way."

7

Lo! glad I come, and Thou bless'd Lamb,
Shalt take me to Thee as I am;
Nothing but Sin I Thee can give,
Nothing but Love shall I receive.

8

Then will I tell to Sinners round,
What a dear Saviour I have found,
I'll point to thy redeeming Blood,
And say," Behold the Way to God".

Dorset

Set by W. B.

How sad our State by Na_ture is Our Sin how

deep it stains And Satan binds our Cap_tive Souls

'Fast in his sla_vish Chains, But there's a Voice of

Sov'reign Grace Sounds from God's sa_ _ _cred Word;

Ho! ye des_ _ pair_ing Sinners, come And trust upon the Lord. Ho! ye des-pairing Sin-ners,

come, And trust up-on the Lord.

2

O may we hear th'Almighty Call,
And run to this Relief!
We would believe thy Promise, Lord,
O help our Unbelief!
To the blest Fountain of thy Blood,
Teach us, O Lord, to fly;
There may we wash our spotted Souls
From Crimes of deepest Dye!

3

Stretch out thine Arm, victorious King,
Our reigning Sins subdue;
Drive the old Dragon from his Seat,
With his infernal Crew.
Poor, guilty, weak, and helpless Worms,
Into thine Hands we fall;
Be Thou our Strength and Righteousness,
Our Jesus and our All!

Wandsworth

Set by M.M.

O Sun of Righteous--ness a--rise,

O Sun of Righteous--ness a--rise,

6 6 6 7 #5

With Heal--ing in thy Wings To

With Heal--ing in thy Wings To

6 6 5
5 4 3

my dis--eas'd my faint--ing Soul

my dis--eas'd my faint--ing Soul

6 6 7 3
5

Thy Light Sal . . . va . . tion brings

(2)

These Clouds of Pride and Sin dispel
By thine all piercing Beam,
Lighten mine Eyes with Faith, my Heart
With holy Hope inflame.

(3)

My Mind by thy all quickning Pow'r
From low Desires set free,
Unite my scatter'd Thoughts, and fix
My Love entire on Thee.

(4)

Father, thy long-lost Son receive;
Saviour, thy Purchase own;
Blest Comforter, with Peace and Joy
Thy new-made Creature crown.

Hotham

Set by M. M.

Jesu, Lover of my Soul, let me to thy

Jesu, Lover of my Soul, let me to thy

Bo-som fly, While the nearer Wa-ters roll, while the

Bo-som fly, While the nearer Wa-ters roll, while the

Tempest still is high; Hide me, O my Saviour, hide,

Tempest still is high; Hide me, O my Saviour, hide,

Till the Storm of Life is past; Safe in-to the

Till the Storm of Life is past; Safe in-to the

2

Other Refuge have I none,
  Hangs my helpless Soul on Thee,
Leave, ah! leave me not alone,
  Still support and comfort me:
All my Trust on Thee is stay'd
  All mine Help from Thee I bring,
Cover my defenceless Head
  With the Shadow of thy Wing.

3

Thou O Christ, art all I want,
  More than All in Thee I find:
Raise the Fallen, cheer the Faint,
  Heal the Sick, and lead the Blind:
Just and Holy is thy Name,
  I am all Unrighteousness!
Vile and full of Sin I am,
  Thou art full of Truth and Grace.

4

Plenteous Grace with Thee is found,
  Grace to pardon all our Sin;
Let the healing Streams abound,
  Make, and keep me pure within.
Thou of Life the Fountain art,
  Freely let me take of Thee,
Spring Thou up within my Heart,
  Rise to all Eternity!

HYMN to the TRINITY

Set by F.G.

Come thou Almigh _ _ty King, Help us thy

Come thou Almigh _ _ty King, Help us thy

6   6

Name   to   sing   Help   us   to   Praise!

Name   to   sing   Help   us   to   Praise!

T.S.

Farther All _ glo _ ri _ ous   O'er All Vic _ to _ ri _ ous!

Farther All _ glo _ ri _ ous   O'er All Vic _ to _ ri _ ous

.5   6   7   .5   6   7
.5   4   .5   .3   1   .5

Come, and reign over us, Antient of Days!

Come, and reign over us, Antient of Days!

2

Jesus our Lord arise,
Scatter our Enemies,
    And make them fall!
Let thine Almighty Aid
Our sure defence be made—
Our Souls on Thee be stay'd
    Lord hear our Call!

3

Come Thou Incarnate Word,
Gird on thy Mighty Sword—
    Our Pray'r attend!
Come,and thy People bless,
And give thy Word success,
Spirit of Holiness
    On us descend!

4

Come Holy Comforter,
Thy Sacred Witness bear,
    In this glad Hour!
Thou who Almighty art,
Now rule in ev'ry Heart,
And ne'er from us depart,
    Spirit of Pow'r!

5

To the Great One in Three
Eternal Praises be
    Hence—Evermore!
His Sov'reign Majesty
May we in Glory see,
And to Eternity
    Love and Adore!

Knightsbridge.

Set by M.M.

Al _ mighty God of Truth and Love! In me thy

Al _ mighty God of Truth and Love! In me thy

Pow'r ex _ _ ert, The Mountain from my Soul re _ _

Pow'r ex _ _ ert, The Mountain from my Soul re _ _

_ move, The Hard _ ness of mine Heart: My Most ob _

_ move, The Hard _ ness of mine Heart: My Most ob _

_ du _ rate Heart sub _ due, In Honour of thy

_ du _ rate Heart sub _ due, In Honour of thy

Son And now the gracious Won-der shew, And take a-- way the Stone. And take a--way the Stone.

Son And now the gracious Won-der shew, And take a-- way the Stone. And take a--way the Stone.

2

I want a Principle within
Of jealous, Godly Fear;
A Sensibility of Sin,
A Pain to feel it near:
I want the first Approach to feel,
Of Pride or vain Desire,
To catch the Wand'rings of my Will,
And quench the kindling Fire.

3

From Thee that I no more may part,
No more thy Goodness grieve;
The filial Awe, the fleshly Heart,
The tender Conscience give:
Quick as the Apple of an Eye,
O God, my Conscience make,
Awake my Soul when sin is nigh,
And keep it still awake!

Rondeau

Set by F.G.

Sweet is the Mem'ry of thy Grace, My God, my hea·ven·ly King! Sweet is &c.

Let Age to Age thy Righ·teous·

- - ness In Sounds of Glo . ry sing.

- - ness In Sounds of Glo ry sing.

2.

God reigns on high, but not confines
His Goodness to the Skies;
Sweet is the Mem'ry of thy Grace,
Thro' the whole Earth his Goodness shines,
And ev'ry want supplies.
Sweet is the Mem'ry of thy Grace.

3

With longing Eye thy Creatures wait
On Thee, for daily Food;
Sweet is the Mem'ry of thy Grace,
Thy lib'ral Hand provides them Meat,
And fills their Mouths with Good.
Sweet is the Mem'ry of thy Grace.

4

How kind, are thy Compassions, Lord!
How slow thine Anger moves!
Sweet is the Mem'ry of thy Grace,
But soon He sends his pard'ning Word,
To chear the Soul He loves.
Sweet is the Mem'ry of thy Grace.

5

Creatures, with all their endless Race,
Thy Pow'r and Praise proclaim;
Sweet is the Mem'ry of thy Grace,
May we, who taste thy richer Grace,
Delight to bless thy Name.
Sweet is the Mem'ry of thy Grace.

Love divine

Love di..vine, all Love ex-cell-ing, Joy of

Love di..vine, all Love ex-cell-ing, Joy of

Heaven to Earth come down! Fix in us thy

Heaven to Earth come down! Fix in us thy

hum-ble dwelling All thy faith-ful Mercies crown

hum-ble dwelling All thy faith-ful Mercies crown

Je--sus Thou art all Com-passion, pure un--

Je--sus Thou art all Com-passion, pure un--

-bound-ed Love Thou art, Vi-sit us with

-bound-ed Love Thou art, Vi-sit us with

thy Sal--va-tion En-ter ev'---ry trembling Heart.

thy Sal--va-tion En-ter ev'---ry trembling Heart,

2

Breathe! O breathe thy loving Spirit,
Into ev'ry troubled Breast!
Let us all in Thee inherit,
Let us find thy promis'd Rest;
Take away the Pow'r of sinning
Alpha and Omega be,
End of Faith, as its Beginning,
Set our Hearts at Liberty.

3

Come! Almighty to deliver,
Let us all thy Life receive!
Suddenly return and never,
Never more thy Temples leave!
Thee we would be always blessing,
Serve thee as thine Hosts above,
Pray, and praise Thee without ceasing,
Glory in thy precious Love.

4

Finish then thy new Creation,
Pure, unspotted may we be,
Let us see thy great Salvation,
Perfectly restor'd by Thee!
Chang'd from Glory into Glory,
'Till in Heaven we take our Place,
'Till we cast our Crowns before Thee,
Lost in Wonder, Love, and Praise.

Beckwith

Bu--ry'd in Sha-dows of the

Bu--ry'd in Sha-dows of the

Night, We lie, 'till Christ re--stores the Light; Wis-

Night, We lie, 'till Christ re--stores the Light; Wis-

--dom de----scends to heal the Blind, And

--dom de--scends to heal the Blind, And

chace the Darkness of the Mind, and chace the

chace the Darkness of the Mind, and chace the

Dark_ness of _ _ _ the Mind.

Dark_ness of _ _ _ the Mind.

2

Lost guilty Souls are drown'd in Tears,
'Till the atoning Blood appears;
Then they awake from deep Distress,
And sing the Lord our Righteousness.

3

Jesus beholds where Satan reigns,
Binding his Slaves in heavy Chains;
He sets the Pris'ner free, and breaks
The iron Bondage from our Necks.

4

Poor helpless Worms in Thee possess
Grace, Wisdom, Pow'r, and Righteousness:
Thou art our mighty All, may we
Give our whole Selves, O Lord, to Thee.

The Penitent

Set by W. B.

Slow

When with my Mind de_vout_ly
When with my Mind de_vout_ly

prest Dear SAVIOUR my re_ _ _ volving Breath
prest Dear SAVIOUR my re_ _ _ volving Breath

Would past Of_ _ fen_ _ces trace Trembling I
Would past Of_ _ fen_ _ces trace Trembling I

make the black re_view Yet pleas'd be_hold ad_
make the black re_view Yet pleas'd be_hold ad_

mir - - ing too the Power the power the

power of chang - ing Grace

2

This Tongue with Blasphemies defil'd,
These Feet to erring Paths beguil'd,
  In Heav'nly League agree,
Who could believe such Lips could praise
Or think my dark and winding ways,
  Should ever lead to Thee.

3

These Eyes that once abus'd their Sight,
Now lift to thee their wat'ry Light,
  And weep a silent Flood,
These Hands ascend in ceaseless Pray'r,
O wash away the Stains they wear,
  In pure redeeming Blood.

4

These Ears that pleas'd could entertain,
The midnight Oath the lustful Strain,
  When round the festal Board,
Now deaf to all th'enchanting Noise,
Avoid the Throng detest the Joys,
  And press to hear thy Word.

5

Thus art Thou serv'd in ev'ry Part,
And now thou dost transform my Heart,
  That drossy Thing refine,
Now Grace doth Nature's Strength confound,
And a new Creature Body Soul,
  Are Lord for ever thine.

Molesworth

Set by W. B.

A _ _ rise my Soul with Won-der see

A _ _ rise my Soul with Won-der see

6
4   6   6   5   7
        4   3

What Love di _ _ vine for thee hath done

What Love di _ _ vine for thee hath done

5 6 5   7 6 5
3 4   4 3

Be _ _ hold thy Sor-row Sin and Grief

Be _ _ hold thy Sor-row Sin and Grief

6   6   5   6   6   6   5
b3 4   =3   4   4 #3

2

See from his Head, his Hands, his Feet,
Sorrow and Love flow mingling down,
Did e'er such Love, such Sorrow meet,
Or Thorns compose so bright a Crown.

3

Were the whole Realm of Nature mine,
That were a Present far too small,
Love so amazing so divine,
Demands my Soul, my Life my All.

Rockingham

Set by *W. B.*

He is a GOD of Sov'reign Love

He is a GOD of Sov'reign Love

That promis'd Heav'n to me And

That promis'd Heav'n to me And

taught my Thoughts to soar a _ _ _ bove

taught my Thoughts to soar a _ _ _ bove

2

Prepare me LORD for thy right Hand
Then come the Joyfull Day
Come Death and some celestial Band
To bear my Soul away.

3

Then my Beloved take my Soul
Up to thy blest Abode
That Face to Face I may behold
My SAVIOUR and my GOD

Helmsley

Lo He comes with Clouds descending Once for favour'd

Lo He comes with Clouds descending Once for favour'd

Sinners slain Thousand thousand Saints attending Swell the

Sinners slain Thousand thousand Saints attending Swell the

Triumph of his Train Hal_le__lujah Hal_le_lu_jah

Triumph of his Train Hal_le__lujah Hal_le_lu_jah

Hal_le_lu_jah Hal__le__lu_jah A___men

Hal_le__lu_jah Hal__le__lu_jah A___men

Ev'ry Eye shall now behold Him,
Rob'd in dreadful Majesty,
Those who set at nought and sold Him,
Pierc'd and nail'd Him to the Tree,
Deeply wailing,
Shall the True MESSIAH see

3

Ev'ry Island Sea, and Mountain,
Heav'n and Earth shall flee away,
All who hate Him, must, confounded,
. Hear the Trump proclaim the Day,
Come to Judgment
Come to Judgment come away

4

Now Redemption long expected,
See in solemn Pomp appear,
All his Saints, by Man rejected,
Now shall meet Him in the Air
Hallelujah
See the Day of GOD appear

5

Answer thine own Bride and Spirit,
Hasten, LORD, the gen'ral Doom
The new Heav'n and Earth t'inherit,
Take thy pining Exiles Home
All Creation
Travails groans and bids Thee come

6

Yea Amen Let all adore Thee,
High on thine eternal Throne
SAVIOUR, take the Pow'r and Glory,
Claim the Kingdom for thine own
O come quickly
Hallelujah Come, LORD come

Dismifsion

F. E.

'Tis Jesus the first and the Last Whose Spirit shall

'Tis Jesus the first and the Last Whose Spirit shall

guide us safe Home We'll praise him for all that is past

guide us safe Home We'll praise him for all that is past

And trust him for all that's to come

And trust him for all that's to come

Pastoral Hymn

Set by J.B.

The LORD my Pas_ture shall pre _ pare

The LORD my Pas_ture shall pre _ pare

And feed me with a Shepherd's Care His presence

And feed me with a Shepherd's Care His presence

shall my wants sup _ _ ply And guard me with a

shall my wants_ sup _ _ ply And guard me with a

watchful Eye My Noon _ day Walks he shall at _ tend

watchful Eye My Noon _ day Walks he shall at _ tend

And all my Mid night Hours de _ fend

And all my Mid night Hours de _ fend

2

When in the sultry Glebe I faint,
Or on the thirsty Mountain pant,
To fertile Vales and dewy Meads,
My weary wand'ring Steps he leads,
Where peaceful Rivers soft and slow,
Amid the verdant Landskip flow.

3

Though in the Path of Death I tread,
With gloomy Horrors overspread,
My stedfast Heart shall fear no Ill,
For thou O LORD art with me still,
Thy friendly Crook shall give me Aid,
And guide me through the dreadful Shade.

4

Tho' in a bare and rugged Way,
Thro' devious lonely Wilds I stray,
Thy Bounty shall my Pains beguile,
The barren Wilderness shall smile,
With sudden Greens and Herbage crown'd.
And Streams shall murmur all around.

Kippax

When I tra-vail in Dis-tress Or Grief of
a--ny Kind Bur-den'd with un-ca---si
--ness Or An-guish on my Mind One sweet

Ray of Heav'nly Light Dis--pels the Clouds which
in-ter--vene Turns to Day the gloo-my
Night And quite re-news the Scene

2

My Complaints with Speed remove,
My Sorrows turn to Joy,
Songs of Melody and Love,
Again my Tongue employ,
Then I find the resting Place,
To all the carnal World unknown,
There I taste the glorious Peace,
Felt by the Saints alone.

Birksted

Slow

Who hath our report be. lieved SHILOH come is not re. ceived Not received by his own Promis'd Branch from Root of Jesse Davids Offspring sent to bless ye Comes too Meekly to be known.

2

Tell me O thou favour'd Nation,
What is thy fond Expectation,
  Some fair spreading lofty Tree,
Let not worldly Pride confound thee,
'Mong the lowly Plants around thee,
  Mark the Lowest that is He.

3

Like a tender Plant that's growing,
Where no Waters friendly flowing,
  No kind Rains refresh the Ground,
Drooping dying we shall view Him,
See no Charms to draw us to Him,
  There no Beauty will be found.

To Messiah unrespected,
MAN of Griefs Despis'd Rejected,
    Wounds his Form disfiguring,
Marr'd His Visage more than any,
For He bears the Sins of Many
    All our Sorrows carrying.

5

No deceit His Mouth had spoken,
Blameless He no Law had broken,
    Yet was number'd with the Worst
For because the LORD would grieve him,
We who saw it did believe Him,
    For his own Offences curst.

6

But while Him our Thoughts accuse'd,
He for Us alone was bruised,
    Striken smitten for Our Guilt,
With His Stripes Our Wounds are cured,
By His Pains Our Peace assured,
    Purchas'd with the Blood He spilt.

7

Love amazing so to mind us,
Shepherd come from Heav'n to find us,
    Silly, Sheep all gone astray,
Lost Undone by our Transgressions,
Worse than stript of all Possessions,
    Debtors without Hope to pay.

8

Fear our Portion Slaves in Spirit,
He redeem'd Us by His Merit,
    To a glorious Liberty,
Dearly first His Goodness bought us,
Truth and Love then sweetly taught us,
    Truth and Love have made us free.

9

Blessed be the Pow'r who gave us,
Freely gave His SON to save us,
    Bless'd the SON who freely came,
Honour Blessing Adoration,
Ever from the whole Creation,
    Be to GOD and to the Lamb.

Chilton

Set by I.B.

Thou GOD of Glorious Majesty to Thee against my self to Thee A Worm of Earth I cry An half a — waken'd Child of Man An Heir of endless Bliss or Pain A Sinner born to die

Lo on a narrow Neck of Land,
'Twixt two unbounded Seas I stand,
Secure insensible,
- A Point of Time a Moment's Space,
Removes me to that heav'nly Place,
Or shuts me up in Hell.

3

O GOD mine inmost Soul convert,
And deeply on my thouhtful Heart,
Eternal Things impress,
Give me to feel their solemn Weight,
And tremble on the Brink of Fate,
And wake to Righteousness.

4

Before me place in dread array,
The Pomp of that tremendous Day,
When Thou with Clouds shall come,
To Judge the Nations at thy Bar,
And tell me LORD shall I be there,
To meet a joyful Doom.

5

Be this my one great Bus'ness here,
With serious industry and Fear,
My future Bliss t'insure,
Thine utmost Counsel to fulfil,
And suffer all thy righteous Will,
And to the End endure.

6

Then SAVIOUR then my Soul receive,
Transported from the Vale to live,
And reign with Thee above,
Where Faith is sweetly lost in Sight,
And Hope in full supreme Delight,
And everlasting Love.

Winwick

Andante

Set by M.M.

O JESU our LORD Thy Name be a--dor'd for
O JESU our LORD Thy Name be a--dor'd for

all the rich Blessings for all the rich Blessings con--
all the rich Blessings for all the rich Blessings con--

--vey'd thro' thy Word con---vey'd thro' thy Word
--vey'd thro' thy Word con---vey'd thro' thy Word

2

In Spirit we trace,
Thy Wonders of Grace,
And chearfully join in a Consort of Praise.

3

The ANTIENT OF DAYS,
His Glory displays,
And shines on his Chosen with cherishing Rays.

4

The Trumpet of GOD,
Is sounding abroad,
The Language of Mercy Salvation thro' Blood.

5

Thrice happy are they,
Who hear and obey,
And share in the Blessing of this Gospel Day.

6

The People who know,
The SAVIOUR below,
With burning Affection to worship Glow.

7

Their Anguish and Smart,
And Sorrows depart,
Who find his Salvation inscrib'd on their Hearts.

8

This Blessing is mine,
Thro' Favour divine,
But O my REDEEMER the glory be thine.

9

The Work is of Grace,
Thine thine be the Praise,
And mine to adore Thee and tell of thy Ways.

Buxton

Set by M.M.

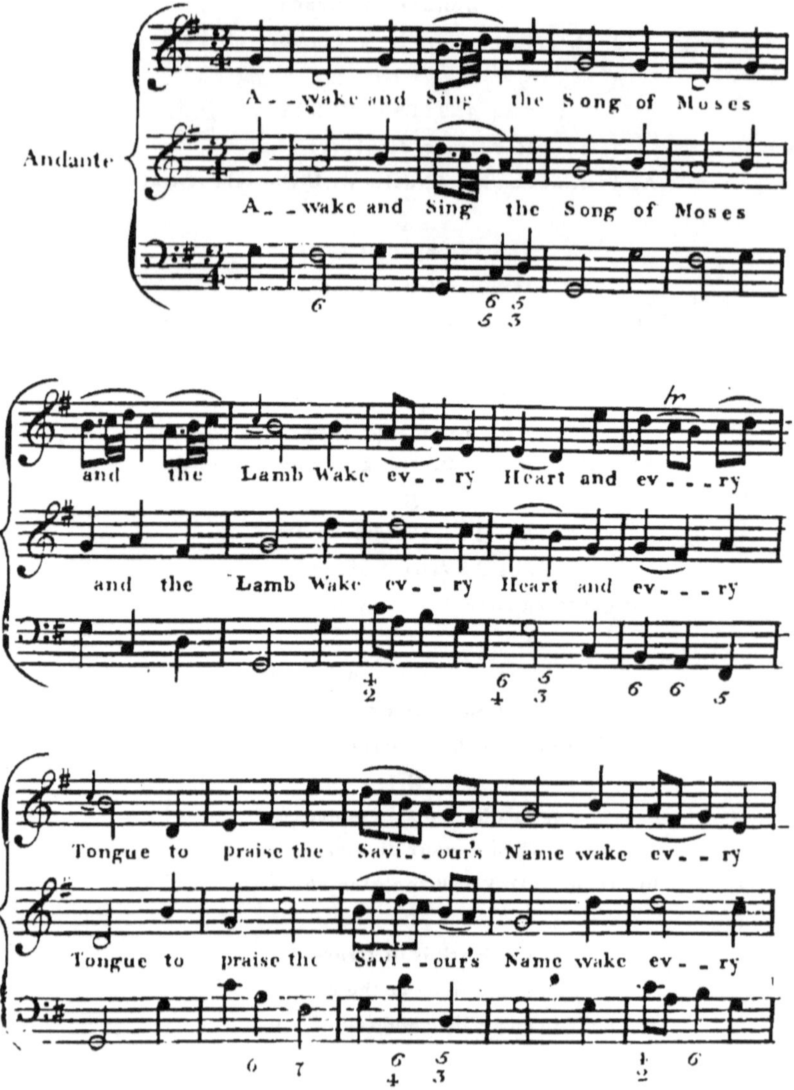

Heart and ev -- ry Tongue to praise the Saviour's Name

Heart and ev -- ry Tongue to praise the Saviour's Name

2
Sing of his dying Love,
Sing of his rising Pow'r,
Sing how He intercedes above,
For those whos Sins He bore.

3
Sing till we feel our Hearts,
Ascending with our Tongues,
Sing till the Love of Sin departs,
And Grace inspires our Song.

4
Sing on your Heav'nly Way,
Ye ransom'd Sinners sing,
Sing on rejoicing ev'ry Day,
In CHRIST th' eternal King.

5
Soon shall ye hear,
Ye blessed Children come,
Soon will He call ye hence away,
And take his Wand'rers home,

Haddersfield

Set by M. M.

Andante

My hid-ing Place my Re-fuge

My hid-ing Place my Re-fuge

Tow'r And Shield art thou O LORD I firm-ly

Tow'r And Shield art thou O LORD I firm-ly

An-chor all my Hopes On thy un-err-ing

An-chor all my Hopes On thy un-err-ing

Word On thy un_ _ err _ ing Word

Word On_ thy un_ _ err _ ing Word

2

Engrav'd as in eternal Brass,
The mighty Promiseshines,
Nor can the Pow'rs of Darkness raze,
Those Everlasting Lines.

3

The Sacred Word of Grace is strong,
As that which built the Skies,
The Voice which rolls the Stars along,
Speak all the Promises.

4

My hiding Place my Refuge Tow'r,
And Shield art thou O LORD,
I firmly anchor all my Hopes,
On thy unerring Word.

Leeds

Andante   Set by M.M.

Je_sus thy Blood and Righte_ous_ness, My

Je_sus thy Blood and Righte_ous_ness, My

Beau__ty are my glori_ous Dress, Midst

Beau__ty are my glori_ous Dress, Midst

flam_ing Worlds in these ar___ray'd With

flam_ing Worlds in these ar___ray'd With

Joy shall I lift up my Head

Joy shall I lift up my Head

2
When from the Dust of Death I rise,
To claim my Mansion in the Skies,
Ev'n then, shall this be all my Plea:
"Jesus hath liv'd hath dy'd for me."

3
Bold shall I stand in that great Day,
For who ought to my Charge shall lay,
Fully thro' Thee absolv'd I am
From Sin and Fear, from Guilt and Shame.

4
Thus Abraham, the Friend of God,
Thus all the Armies bought with Blood,
Saviour of Sinners Thee proclaim,
Sinners, of whom the Chief I am.

5
This spotless Robe the same appears,
When ruin'd Nature sinks in Years;
No Age can change its glorious Hue,
The Grace of Christ is ever new.

6
O let the Dead now hear thy Voice,
Now bid thy banish'd Ones rejoice,
Their Beauty this, their glorious Dress,
Jesus, the Lord our Righteousness.

Richmond.

Andante

Set by M.M.

When I sur.vey _ _d the wond'rous Cross, On

When I sur.vey _ _d the wond'rous Cross, On

6   7   6   6 5
                                 4 3

which   the   Prince   of   Glo _ _ _ ry   dy'd,   My

which   the   Prince   of   Glo _ _ _ ry   dy'd,   My

7   6 5
           4 3

rich _ _ est   Gain   I   count   but   Loss, — And

rich _ _ est   Gain   I   count   but   Loss,   And

7   6   7   6 5
                      5   4 3

pour   Con _ _ tempt   on   all   my   Pride

pour   Con _ _ tempt   on   all   my   Pride

pour   Con _ _ tempt   on   all   my   Pride

6 7
6   5
4   5

all my Pride My rich - - est Gain I
all my Pride My rich - - est Gain I

count . but Loss, And pour Con - - tempt on
count but Loss, And pour Con - - - tempt on

all my Pride all my Pride
all my Pride all my Pride
all my Pride all my Pride

2

Forbid it Lord, that I should boast,
Save in the Cross of Christ, my God:
All the vain Things that charm me most,
I sacrifice them for thy Blood.

REDEEMING LOVE

Set by I. W.

Now be-gin the Heav'nly Theme, Sing a-loud in Je-su's Name, Sing a-loud in Je-su's Name Ye who Je-su's Kindness prove, Triumph in Re-deem-ing Love

Octaves

Triumph in Re-deem-ing Love

Triumph in Re-deem-ing Love

2

Ye who see the Father's Grace,
Beaming in the Saviour's Face,
As to Canaan on ye move
Praise and bless Redeeming Love.

3

Mourning Sons dry up your Tears,
Banish all your guilty Fears,
See your Guilt and Curse remove,
Cancell'd by Redeeming Love.

4

Ye alas! who long have been,
Willing Slaves of Death and Sin,
Now from Bliss no longer rove,
Stop — and taste Redeeming Love.

5

Welcome all by Sin opprest,
Welcome, to his sacred Rest,
Nothing brought Him from above,
Nothing but Redeeming Love.

6

He subdu'd th'Infernal Pow'rs,
His tremendous Foes and ours,
From their cursed Empire drove,
Mighty in Redeeming Love.

7

Hither then your Music bring,
Strike aloud each joyful String,
Mortals join the Hosts above,
Join to praise Redeeming Love.

Scarborough

What shall we render un - - - to Thee, Thou glorious Lord of
Life and Pow'r! Teach us to bow the humble knee, Teach us with Thankfull-
-ness t'adore; To praise Thee to praise Thee as the Hosts a-bove,
To praise Thee to praise Thee for thy wond'rous Love

When like lost Sheep we wander'd wide,
　　And left the watchful Shepherd's Eye;
When borne along th'impetuous Tide,
　　Of this Word's Sin and Vanity;
　　　Our Jesus from the Heavens came down,
　　　To save us by his Grace alone.

3

He bore our Sins upon the Tree
　. To seek and save the lost He came
There was He bound to set us free
　　From Death and everlasting Shame;
　　　The captive Flock from Hell was freed,
　　　And ransom'd when theis Shepherd bled.

4

Before the Father's awfull Throne;
　　Our mercifull High—Priest, He stands,
And interceding for his own,
　　The purchas'd Remnant now Demands,
　　　His People's everlasting Friend,
　　　Who loving—loves them to the End.

5

May we his banish'd ones rejoice,
　　Him for our Lord and God to own,
To take Him as our only Choice,
　　And cleave to Him in Love, alone;
　　　Be growing up in Holiness,
　　　Then meet him in the Realms of Peace.

6

Then shall our grateful Songs abound,
　　And ev'ry Tear be wip'd away;
No Sin, No Sorrow shall be found,
　, No Night o'er-cloud the endless Day.
　　　O Praise Him! all beneath, above,
　　　O Praise Him! Praise the God of Love!

Brighthelmston

Andante

O Lord, how great's the Favour! That we such Sinners poor,

Lord, how great's the Favour! That we such Sinners poor,

6   ×   ♯   6   ♯ 6   ♯   6   7   ♯

Can thro' thy Blood's sweet savour, Ap - -proach thy Mercy's Door,

Can thro' thy Blood's sweet savour, Ap - -proach thy Mercy's Door,

6   ×   5   ♯   6   6   —   6   7   ♯

To find an open Passage, Un - to the Throne of Grace, There

To find an open Passage, Un - to the Throne of Grace, There

3   6 9   6   9   7   5   4 7   7   5

wait the Welcome Message, That bids us go in Peace, There

wait the Welcome Message, That bids us go in Peace, There

6 9   6   6 5   ♯   6   6 5   1   4   3   4 3

wait the Welcome Mes-sage That bids us go in Peace.

wait the Welcome Mes-sage That bids us go in Peace.

(2)

Lord, we are helpless Creatures,
  Full of the deepest Need,
Throughout defil'd by Nature,
  Stupid, and inly Dead;
Our Strength is perfect Weakness,
  And all we have is Sin,
Our Hearts are all Uncleaness,
  A Den of Thieves within.

(3)

In this forlorn Condition,
  Who shall afford us Aid!
Where shall we find Compassion,
  But in the Church's Head.
Jesus, thou art all Pity,
  O take us to thine Arms,
And exercise thy Mercy,
  To saves us from all Harms.

(4)

We'll never cease repeating
  Our numberless Complaints,
But ever be intreating
  The glorious King of Saints;
Till we attain the Image
  Of Him we inly love,
And pay our grateful Homage
  With all the Saints above.

(5)

Then we, with all in Glory,
  Shall thankfully relate
Th'amazing, pleasing Story,
  Of Jesu's Love so great:
In this blest Contemplation
  We shall for ever dwell,
And prove such Consolation
  As none below can tell.

Chelsea

Set by W. B.

With Joy we me-di-'tate the Grace Of our

With Joy we me-di-tate the Grace Of our

High—Priest a-bove; His Heart is made of Ten-der-

High—Priest a-bove His Heart is made of Ten-der-

--ness, His Bowels melt with Love. His Heart is made of

--ness, His Bowels melt with Love. His Heart is made of

Ten_der_ness, His Bow_els melt with Love.

Ten_der_ness, His Bow_els melt with Love.

2

Touch'd with a Sympathy within,
He knows our feeble Frame:
He knows what sore Temptations mean,
For He hath felt the same.

3

He, in the Days of feeble Flesh,
Pour'd out his Cries and Tears,
And in his Measure feels afresh,
What every Member bears.

4

He'll never quench the smoaking Flax,
But raise it to a Flame,
The bruised Reed He never breaks,
Nor scorns the meanest Name.

5

Then let our humble Faith address,
His Mercy and his Pow'r
We shall obtain deliv'ring Grace
In the distressing Hour.

Waybridge

Set by M.M.

Lord where shall guil-ty Souls re-tire For-
Lord where shall guil-ty Souls re-tire For-

-got-ten and un--known In Hell they
-got-ten and un--known In Hell they

meet thy vengefull Ire In Heav'n thy glorious
meet thy vengefull Ire In Heav'n thy glorious

Throne. In Heav'n thy glorious Throne.

Throne. In Heav'n thy glorious Throne.

2

Should they suppress their vital Breath,
T'escape the Wrath Divine,
Thy Voice would break the Bars of Death,
And make the Grave resign.

3

If wing'd with Beams of Morning Light
They fly beyond the West,
Thine Hand, which must support their Flight,
Would soon betray their Rest.

4

If o'er their Sins they seek to draw
The Curtains of the Night,
Those flaming Eyes that guard thy Law,
Would turn the Shades to Light.

5

The Beams of Noon, the Midnight Hour,
Are both alike to Thee;
O may we ne'er provoke that Pow'r
From which we cannot flee!

HYMN of Thanksgiving for Deliverance in a Storm.

STADE

Set by I. B.

Our lit_tle Bark on boist'rous Seas

Our lit_tle Bark on boist'rous Seas

By cru_el Tempest tost With_out one

By cru_el Tempest tost With_out one

chearfull Beam of Hope Ex_pecting to be lost

chearfull Beam of Hope Ex_pecting to be lost

(NB: The Hallelujah, to be Sung only at the End of the 5.th & 6.th Verses.)

Hal_le__lujah Halle lujah Halle__lujah A___men.

Hal_le__lujah Halle lujah Halle__lujah A___men.

2

We to the Lord in Humble Pray'r
Breath'd out our sad Distress
Tho' feeble, Yet with contrite Hearts
We beg'd return of Peace.

3

With pitying Eyes, the Prince of Grace,
Beheld our helpless Grief;
He saw, and (O amazing Love)!
"He came to our Relief."

4

The Stormy Winds did cease to blow
The Waves no more did roll
And soon again a placid Sea
Spoke Comfort to each Soul.

5

Oh! may our gratefull, trembling Hearts
Sweet Hallelujahs sing
To Him, who hath our lives preserv'd
Our Saviour and our King.

6

Let us proclaim to all the World
With Heart and Voice again
And tell the Wonders he hath done
For us the Sons of Men.

Heighinton

Altered from Dr. H.

Sal - va - - tion! O the joy - - ful Sound! What

Sal - va - - tion! O the joy - - ful Sound! What

Pleasure to our Ears! A sov' - - rein

Pleasure to our Ears! A sov' - - rein

Balm for ev' - ry Wound, A Cor - - dial

Balm for ev' - ry Wound, A Cor - - dial

for our Fears. A sov'-reign Balm for ev'--ry

for our Fears. A sov'-reign Balm for ev'--ry

Wound, A Cor-dial for our Fears.

Wound, A Cor-dial for our Fears.

(2)

Salvation! let the Ec-ho fly

The spacious Earth around

While all the Armies of the Sky

Conspire to raise the Sound.

German

O Come, thou wounded Lamb of God! Come,
wash us in thy cleans - - - ing Blood, Give
us to know thy Love, then Pain Is

sweet, and Life or Death is Gain.

sweet, and Life or Death is Gain.

6   6 #6   #4   6   6   5
                b3   4   X

2
Take our poor Hearts, and let them be
For ever clos'd to all but Thee:
Seal Thou our Breasts, and let us wear
That Pledge of Love for ever there.

3
How can 'it be, thou Heav'nly King
That thou should'st Man to Glory bring!
Make Slaves the Partners of thy Throne,
Deck'd with a never—fading Crown!

4
Ah. Lord! enlarge our scanty Thought,
To know the Wonders thou hast wrought,
Unloose our stamm'ring Tongue to tell
Thy Love immense, unsearchable.

5
First-born of many Brethren Thou,
To Thee both Earth and Heav'n must bow;
Help us to Thee our All we give,
Thine may we die, thine may we live.

LOCK HOSPITAL

A New

AND

IMPROVED EDITION OF

The Collection of

PSALM & HYMN TUNES,

SUNG

at the CHAPEL of the

LOCK HOSPITAL.

Book 2

Price

London

Printed by Broderip & Wilkinson, 13 Hay-market

Where are Printed the 1st 2nd 3rd & 4th Books of the Magdalen Hymns, 2s each

INDEX

BOOK 2d

Hallifax

Set by M. M.

Ho, ev'ry one that thirsts, draw.

nigh, ('Tis God in_vites the fal__len Race)

Mer_cy and free Sal___va_tion buy, Buy

Wine, and Milk, and Gosple— Grace.

Wine, and Milk, and Gosple— Grace.

2

Come to the living Waters, come,
Sinners, obey your Maker's Call,
Return, ye weary Wand'rers home
And find my Grace reach'd out to all.

3

See, from the Rock a Fountain rise,
For you in healing Streams it rolls;
Money ye need not bring, nor Price,
Ye lab'ring burthen'd, Sin-sick Souls.

4

Nothing ye in Exchange shall give;
Leave all you have, and are, behind;
Frankly the Gift of God receive,
Pardon, and Peace, in Jesus find.

Windsor ·

Set by M.M.

Andante

The Lord of Sabbath   let us praise In Concert with the

The Lord of Sabbath   let us praise In Concert with the

6   6

Blest, Who Joyful   in harmonious   Lays Employ an

Blest, Who Joyful   in harmonious   Lays Employ an

6   6

end-lefs Rest employ an endless Rest.   Who Joyful in har_

end-lefs Rest employ an endless Rest.   Who Joyful in har_

_ monious Lays Em- ploy an endless Rest.

_ monious Lays Em- ploy an endless Rest.

6   6   6   5
                         4   3

2

Thus, Lord, while we remember Thee,
We blest and pious grow;
By Hymns of Praise we learn to be,
Triumphant here below.

3

On this glad Day a brighter Scene,
Of Glory was display'd,
By God, th'eternal Word, than when
This Universe was made.

4

He rises, who Mankind hath bought
With Grief and Pain extreme;
'Twas great to speak the World from Nought —
'Twas greater to redeem!

Milbank

Set by C.B.

Of him who did Sal_va___tion bring,

Of him who did Sal_va__tion bring,

Lord, may we e__ver think and sing! A_

Lord, may we e__ver think and sing! A_

_rise, ye guil_ty he'll for__give; A_

_rise, ye guil_ty he'll for__give; A_

_ rise ye nee _ _ dy he'll re _ _ lieve.

_ rise ye nee _ _ dy he'll re _ _ lieve.

2

Eternal Lord, Almighty King
All Heav'n doth with thy triumphs ring!
Thou conquer'st all beneath, above,
Devils with force, and Men with Love!

3

To purge our Sins, Christ shed his Blood,
He dy'd to bring us near to God:
Let all the World fall down and know,
That none but God such Love could show.

Plymouth.

Set by M. V.

O God our Help in A - ges past, Our Hope for Years for

O God our Help in A - ges past, Our Hope for Years for

6 6 7 6 6   3 6 5   6.
      5 4   4 3

Years to come, Our Shel - ter from the stor - my Blast,

Years to come, Our Shel - ter from the stor - my Blast,

6 7   6 5   7 6 5   6 6   7   7
       4 3   5 4 3

And our e - ter - nal e - ternal Home. Be - fore the Hills in

And our e - ter - nal e - ternal Home. Be - fore the Hills in

5 6 5   6 6   6   6 5   7
        4 4   3   #3

Or - der stood, Or Earth re - ceiv'd re - ceiv'd its Frame, From

Or - der stood, Or Earth re - ceiv'd re - ceiv'd its Frame, From

6   6   7   9 6 7
3   5   5   7 8
    4 3

e _ ver las _ ting thou art God. To end _ lefs end _ lefs

e _ ver las _ ting thou art God. To end _ lefs end _ lefs

Years the fame. To end _ lefs end _ lefs Years the fame.

Years the fame. To end _ lefs end _ lefs Years the fame.

2

A thousand Ages in thy Sight
Are as an Ev'ning gone
Short as the Watch that ends the Night
Before the rising Sun.

3

The busy Tribes of Flesh and Blood,
With all their Cares and Fears,
Are carry'd downward by the Flood,
And lost in foll'wing Years.

Edgcumbe.

Set by W. B.

My drowsy Pow'rs why sleep ye so? A-wake, my sluggish Soul: Nothing hath half thy Work to do; Yet nothing's half so dull Yet nothing's half so dull.

nothing's half so dull.

(2)

Go to the Ants—for one poor Grain,
  See how they toil and strive;
Yet·we who have Heav'n t' obtain,
  How negligent we live.

(3)

We for whom God the Son came down,
  And labour'd for our Good;
How careless to secure that Crown,
  He purchas'd with his Blood.

(4)

Lord shall we live so sluggish still,
  And never act our Parts;
Come Lord thy gracious Word fulfil,
  And warm our frozen Hearts.

(5)

Give us with active Warmth to move,
  With vig'rous Souls to rise;
With Hands of Faith and Wings of Love,
  To fly and take the Prize.

Turin.

Set by F.G.

Son of God! thy Blessing grant Still sup‿ply my

Son of God! thy Blessing grant Still sup‿ply my

ev'ry Want, Tree of Life thine Influence shed,

ev'ry Want, Tree of Life thine Infuence shed,

With thy Sap my Spirit feed, With thy Sap my

With thy Sap my Spirit feed, With thy Sap my

Spirit feed, With thy Sap my Sipirit feed.

Spirit feed, With thy Sap my Sipirit feed.

2

Tend'rest Branch, alas! am I,
Wither without Thee, and die:
Weak as helpless Infancy
O confirm my Soul in Thee.

3

Unsustain'd by Thee I fall,
Send the Strength for which I call!
Weaker than a bruised Reed,
Help I ev'ry Moment need.

4

All my Hopes on thee depend,
Love me! save me to the End!
Give me the continuing Grace
Take the everlasting Praise.

Bramham.

Set by F.G.

O tell me no more of this Worlds vain

O tell me no more of this Worlds vain

6   6   5   6   5
    4   4   3

Store: The Time for such Tri_fles the Time for such

Store: The Time for such Tri_fles the Time for such

7

Tri_fles the Time for such Tri_fles, With me now is

Tri_fles the Time.for such Tri_fles, With me now is

6   6   6   5
4   4   3

Under the music staves, the lyrics beneath the notes:

o'er With me now is o'er.

o'er With me now is o'er.

2

A Country I've found,
Where true joys abound:
To dwell I'm determin'd
On that happy Ground.

3

The Souls that believe,
In Paradise live
And me in that Number
Will Jesus receive.

4

My Soul don't delay,
He calls thee away;
Rise, follow thy Saviour,
And bless the glad Day.

5

No Mortal doth know
What He can bestow,
What Light, Strength,& Comfort;
Go after Him, go.

6

And when I'm to die,
Receive me, I'll cry,
For Jesus hath lov'd me,
I cannot say why.

7

And now I'm in Care
My Neighbours may share
These Blessings: To seek them
Will none of you dare.

8

In Bondage O why!
And Death will you lie,
When One here assures you
Free Grace is so nigh

Canterbury.

Set by I. W.

Hail great Im__ma_nuel! bal__my
Hail great Im__ma_nuel! bal__my

5 — 6
6 — 5 3
4 — 3 8

Name thy Praise the ran_som'd will pro_
Name thy Praise the ran_som'd will pro_

6
6
5
7
3

claim. We thee Phy__si__cian call We own no
claim.   We own no

6
b3 6

o‑‑‑ther cure but thine; Thou the de‑

o‑‑‑ther cure but thine; Thou the de‑

‑li‑‑verer‑‑‑ di‑‑‑‑vine! our

‑li‑‑verer‑‑‑ di‑‑‑‑vine! our

Health! our life our all

Health! our life our all

Yarmouth.

Set by I. W.

Come ye that love the Lord, And let your Joys be known,

Come ye that love the Lord, And let your Joys be known,

Join in a Song with sweet Accord, While ye surround the Throne, The

Join in a Song with sweet Accord, While ye surround the Throne, The

Sorrows of the Mind Be banish'd from the Place; Re--

Sorrows of the Mind Be banish'd from the Place; Re--

_ _ligion never was design'd To make our Pleasures less. Re-

_ _ligion never was design'd To make our Pleasures less. Re-

(2)

Let those refuse to sing
Who never knew our God;
But Children of the heav'nly King
Will speak their joys abroad.

(3)

The Men of Grace have found
Glory begun below;
Celestial Fruits, on earthly Ground,
From Faith and Hope may grow.

(4)

The Hill of Zion yields
A thousand sacred Sweets,
Before we reach the heav'nly Fields
Or walk the golden Streets.

(5)

Then let our Songs abound,
And every Tear be dry
We're marching thro' Immanuel's Ground
To fairer Worlds on high.

Feversham.

Set by M.M.

Come let us as cend, My Companion and Friend, To a

Come let us as cend, My Companion and Friend, To a

6   5   6   6   6   5   6
                        4   3

Taste of the Ban - quet a bove, If thine Heart be as

Taste of the Ban - quet a bove, If thine Heart be as

6   6   5

mine, If for Je - sus it pine, Come up in - to the

mine, If for Je - sus it pine, Come up in - to the

6   6   5   6   8   7   6   9   7
    4   3   5   6   5.
                    #

Chariot of Love, Come up in_to the Chariot of Love.

Chariot of Love, Come up in_to the Chariot of Love.

2

Who in Jesus confide,
They are bold to outride
The Storms of Affliction beneath;
With the Prophet they soar
To that heav'nly Shore,
And outfly all the Arrows of Death.

3

By Faith we are come
To our permanent Home,
By Hope we the Rapture improve;
By Love we still rise,
And look down on the Skies
For the Heav'n of Heavens is Love!

4

Who on Earth can conceive
How happy we live
In the City of God the great King!
What a Concert of Praise,
When our Jesus's Grace,
The whole heavenly Company sing!

5

What a rapturous Song
When the glorify'd Throng,
In the Spirit of Harmony join!
Join all the glad Choirs,
Hearts, Voices and Lyres,
And the Burthen is Mercy divine.

6

Hallelujah they cry
To the King of the Sky,
To the great everlasting I am,
To the Lamb that was slain,
And liveth again,
Hallelujah to God and the Lamb.

Pelham

My Soul repeat his Praise, Whose Mercies are so great; Whose Anger is so slow to rise, So ready to abate. High as the Heav'ns are rais'd above the Ground we tread, So far the Rich_es of his Grace, Our highest thoughts ex-

far the Rich_es of his Grace, Our highest thoughts ex-

_ceed. Our high_est thoughts ex_ ceed.

_ceed. Our high_est thoughts ex_ ceed.

3

The Pity of the Lord,
  To those that fear his Name,
Is such as tender Parents feel:
  He knows our feeble Frame.

4

Our Days are as the Grass,
  Or like the Morning Flow'r;
If one sharp Blast sweep o'er the Field,
  It withers in an Hour.

5

But thy Compassions, Lord,
  To endless Years endure;
And Children's Children ever find
  Thy Word of Promise sure,
My Soul, repeat his Praise,
  Whose Mercies are so great &c.

Shaftesbury

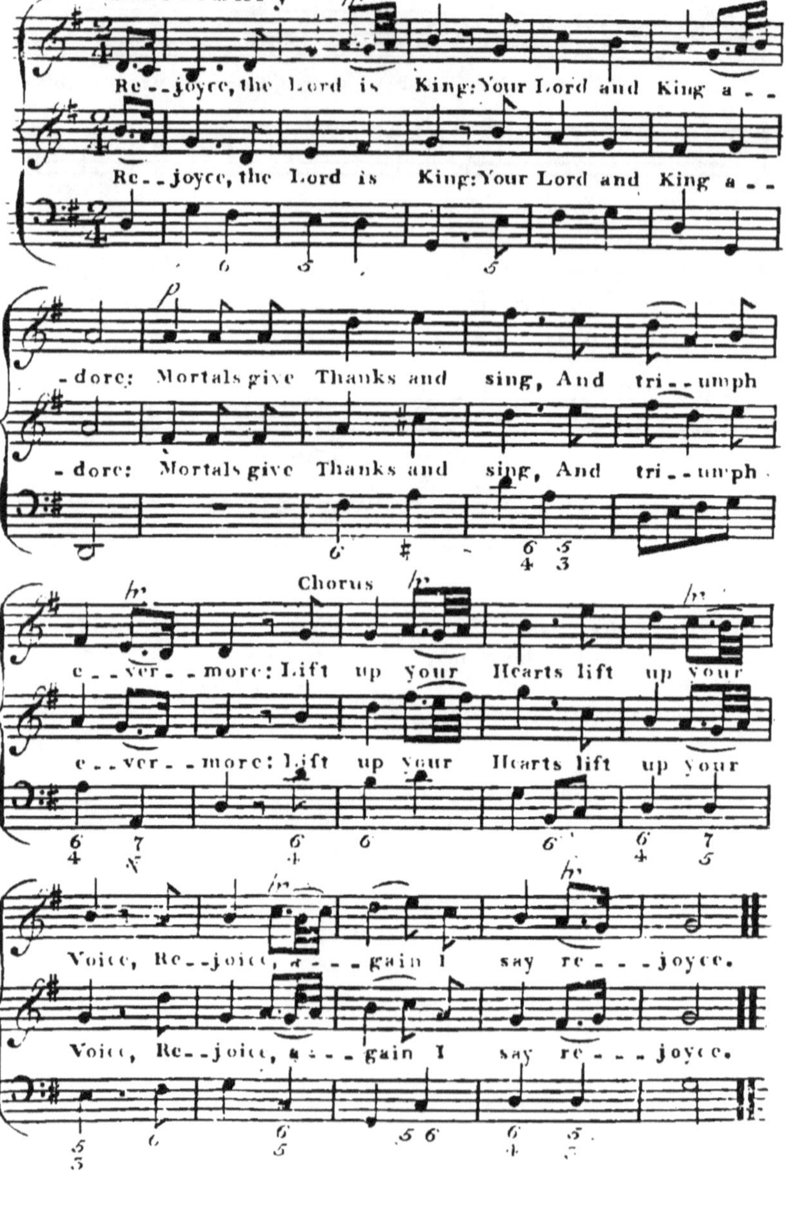

Jesus the Saviour reigns,
   The God of Truth and Love;
When he had purg'd our Stains,
   He took his Seat above:
Lift up your Hearts, lift up your Voice,
   Rejoice, again I say, Rejoice.

3

His Kingdom cannot fail,
   He rules o'er Earth and Heav'n:
The Keys of Death and Hell
   Are to our Jesus giv'n:
Lift up your Hearts, lift up your Voice,
   Rejoice, again I say, Rejoice.

4

He sits at God's Right Hand,
   Till all his Foes submit,
And bow to his Command,
   And fall beneath his Feet:
Lift up your Hearts, lift up your Voice,
   Rejoice, again I say, Rejoice.

5

He all his Foes shall quell,
   Shall all our Sins destroy,
And ev'ry Bosom swell,
   With pure seraphic Joy:
Lift up your Hearts, lift up your Voice,
   Rejoice, again I say, Rejoice.

6

Rejoice in glorious Hope,
   Jesus the Judge shall come,
And take his Servants up
   To their Eternal Home:
We soon shall hear th'Archangel's Voice,
The Trump of God shall sound, Rejoice.

Shrewsbury.

Set by M. V.

Holy Lamb, who Thee re-ceive, Who in Thee be-gin to

Holy Lamb, who Thee re-ceive, Who in Thee be-gin to

live, Day and Night they cry to Thee, As Thou art, so

live, Day and Night they cry to Thee, As Thou art, so

let us be. Fix, O fix each wav'ring Mind, To thy

let us be. Fix, O fix each wav'ring Mind, To thy

Cross our Spirit bind; Earthly Passion far re-move,

Cross our Spirit bind; Earthly Passion far re-move,

Perfect all our Souls in Love.

Perfect all our Souls in Love.

4

Dust and Ashes tho' we be
Full of Guilt and Misery;
Thine we are, thou Son of God!
Take the Purchase of thy Blood.

5

Boundless Wisdom, Pow'r divine,
Love unspeakable are Thine;
Praise by all to Thee be giv'n
Sons of Earth and Hosts of Heav'n.

Dartmouth.

Set by C.B.

We give immortal Praise, immortal Praise To God the

We give immortal Praise, immortal Praise To God the

Fa_ther's Love; For all our Comforts here And

Fa_ther's Love; For all our Comforts here And

better Hopes a_bove, and better Hopes a bove.

better Hopes a_bove, and better Hopes a bove.

He sent his own e_ternal Son, To die for Sins that

He sent his own e_ternal Son, To die for Sins that

Man had done, To die for Sins that Man had done.

Man had done, To die for Sins that Man had done.

(2)

To God the Son belongs
Immortal Glory too,
Who bought us with his Blood,
From everlasting Woe:
    And now he lives
    And now he reigns,
    And sees the Fruit
    Of all his Pains.

(3)

To God the Spirit's Name
Immortal Worship give;
Whose new creating Pow'r
Makes the dead Sinner live;
    His Work completes
    The great Design,
    And fills the Soul
    With Joy divine.

(4)

Almighty God, to Thee
Be endless Honours done;
The undivided Three
And the mysterious One.

    Where Reason fails
    With all her Pow'rs
    There faith prevails
    And love adores.

Almighty God to Thee to Thee

Montpellier. Set by I. B.

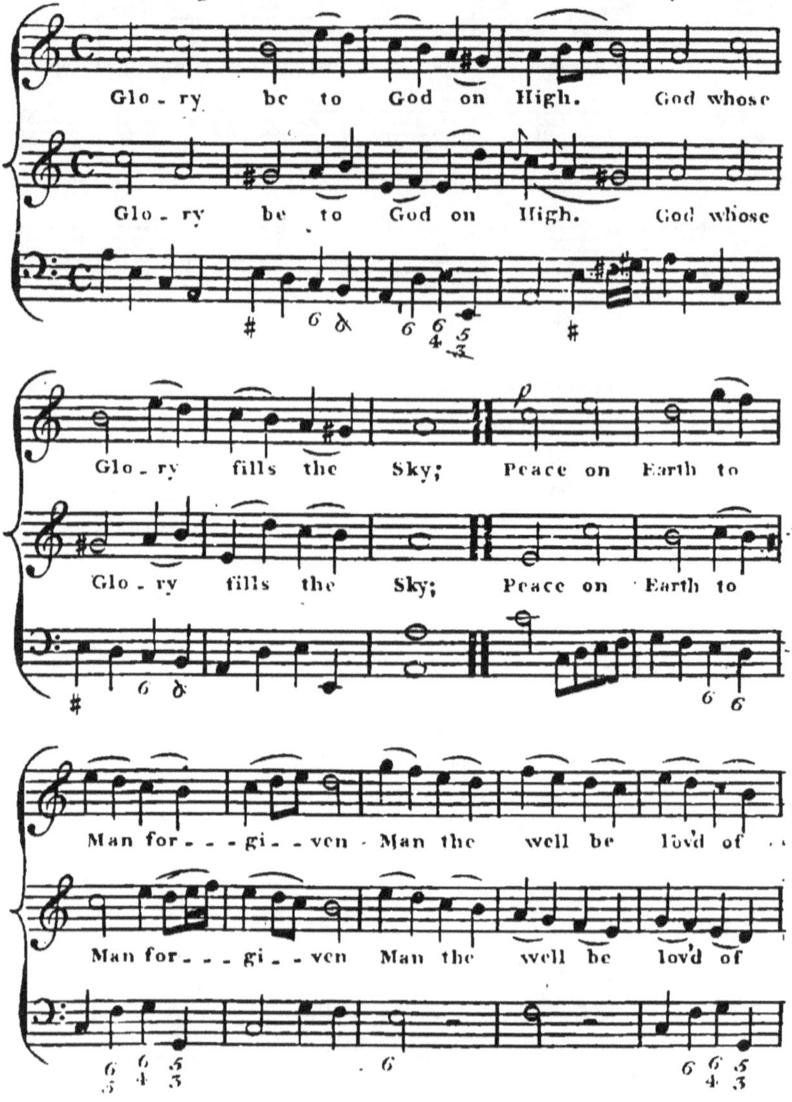

Chorus

Heav'n Glo _ ry be to God on high.

Heav'n Glo _ ry be to God on high.

God whose Glo _ _ ry fills the Sky.

God whose Glo _ _ ry fills the Sky.

2

Christ our Lord and God we own,
Christ the Father's only Son,
Lamb of God for Sinners flain
Saviour of offending Man. Chorus
Glory be to God on high. &c.

Xmas

Set by M.M.

Lift up your Heads in joy-full Hope, Sa-lute the hap-py

Lift up your Heads in joy-full Hope, Sa-lute the hap-py

Morn; Sa-lute the hap-py Morn; Each Heav'nly Pow'r pro-

Morn; Sa-lute the hap-py Morn; Each Heav'nly Pow'r pro-

-claims the glad Hour, Lo! Jesus the Saviour is born. Lo Jesus the

-claims the glad Hour, Lo! Jesus the Saviour is born. Lo Jesus the

Saviour is born.

Saviour is born.

9 8 6 5
7 6 4 3

(2)

All Glory be to God on high,
To Him all Praise is due;
The Promise is feal'd,
The Saviour's reveal'd,
And proves that the Record is true.
(3)
Let Joy around like Rivers flow,
Flow on, and still increase;
Spread o'er the glad Earth,
At Jesus his Birth,
For Heaven and Earth are at Peace.

(4)

Now the Good-will of Heaven is fhewn,
Tow'rds Adams helpless Race,
Meffiah is come
To ransom his Own,
To save them by infinite Grace.
(5)
Then let us join the Heavens above
Where hymning Seraphs sing,
Join all the glad Pow'rs,
For their Lord is Ours,
Our Prophet, our Priest, and our King.

Berwick.

Set by M.M.

Thou dear Redeemer, dying Lamb, We love to

Thou dear Redeemer, dying Lamb, We love to

hear of Thee, No Music like thy charming Name, Nor

hear of Thee, No Music like thy charming Name, Nor

half nor half so sweet can be. nor

half nor half so sweet can be. nor

half nor half so sweet can be.

half nor half so sweet can be.

2

O may we ever hear thy Voice,
   In Mercy to us speak,
And in our Prieft will we rejoice,
   Thou great Melchifedec.

3

Our Jesus shall be still our Theme,
   While in this World we stay,
We'll fing our Jefu's lovely Name,
   When all Thing elfe decay.

4.

When we appear in yonder Cloud,
   With all his favour'd Throng,
Then will we fing more sweet more loud,
   And Chrift fhall be our Song.

Fordwich

C. B.

What shall we render un to Thee Thou glorious

What shall we render un to Thee Thou glorious

Lord of Life and Pow'r! Teach us to bow the hum..ble

Lord of Life and Pow'r! Teach us to bow the hum..ble

Knee Teach us teach us with Thank-ful..nefs t' a dore;

Knee Teach us teach us with Thank-ful..nefs t' a dore;

To praise thee as the Saints a bove, To praise thee

To praise thee as the Saints a bove, To praise thee

for thy wond'rous Love, To praise thee for thy wond'rous Love.

for thy wond'rous Love, To praise thee for thy wond'rous Love.

2

When like lost Sheep, we wander'd wide,
And left the watchful Shepherd's Eye;
When borne along th'impetuous Tide,
Of this World's Sin and Vanity;
Our Jesus from the Heav'ns came down,
To fave us by his Grace alone.

3

He bore our Sins upon the Tree
(To seek and save the lost He came)
There was He bound to set us free
From Death and everlasting Shame:
The captive Flocks from Hell was freed,
And ransom'd when their Shepherd bled.

4

Before the Father's awful Throne;
Our merciful High-Priest, he stands,
And interceding for his own,
The purchas'd Remnant now demands,
His People's everlasting Friend,
Who, loving-loves them to the End.

5

May we, his banish'd ones rejoice,
Him for our Lord and God to own,
To take Him as our only Choice,
And cleave to Him, in Love, alone;
Be growing up in Holiness,
Then meet Him in the Realms of Peace.

6

Then shall our grateful Songs abound,
And ev'ry Tear be wip'd away;
No Sin no Sorrow shall be found,
No Night o'er-cloud the endless Day.
Oh praise Him! all beneath above,
Oh praise Him! Praise the God of Love!

Reading.

Set by T. H.

Je-su
my Saviour in thy Face the Essence lives of ev'-ry Grace.

All things besides which charm the Sight are shadows tipt with

Glow__worm light are fhadows tipt__with Glowworm Light.

Thy beauty Lord th'enrapturd

Eye which ful__ly views it first must die then let me die thro'

Death to know that Joy I seek in vain below that Joy I seek in

vain below

Sheldon

Hap - - - - py the Heart, where Gra - - ces reign,
Hap - - - - py the Heart, where Gra - - ces reign,
Where Love in - - - spires the Breast Love
Where Love in - - - spires the Breast Love
is - - - - the Bright - - est of - - - - the Train,
is - - - - the Bright - - est of - - - - the Train.

And per fects all the rest.

And per fects all the rest.

2

Knowledge, alas! 'tis all in vain,
    And all in vain our Fear:
Our stubborn Sins will fight and reign,
    If Love be absent there.

3

'Tis Love that makes our chearful feet
    In swift Obedience move:
The Devils know and tremble too—
    But Satan cannot love.

4

This is the Grace that lives and sings,
    When Faith and Hope shall cease;
'Tis this shall strike our joyful Strings,
    In the sweet Realms of Blifs.

5

When join'd to that harmonious Throng,
    That fills the Choirs above,
Then shall we tune our golden Harps
    And ev'ry Note be— Love.

Lancaster

Set by M.M.

Praise the Lord, who reigns a_bove, And keeps his Court be-

Praise the Lord, who reigns a_bove, And keeps his Court be-

_low, Praise the ho_ly God of Love, And all his Greatness

_low, Praise the ho_ly God of Love, And all his Greatness

fhow Praife Him for his no_ble Deeds, Praise Him for his

fhow Praife Him for his no_ble Deeds, Praise Him for his

matchlefs Pow'r; Him from whom all Good pro. ceeds, Let Heav'n

matchlefs Pow'r; Him from whom all Good pro. ceeds, Let Heav'n

6 ♯6   6   6   6   7 6   7

and Earth a .dore. Let Heav'n and Earth a _ _ dore.

and Earth a.dore. Let Heav'n and Earth a _ _ dore.

and Earth a.dore. Let Heav'n and Earth a _ _ dore.

6   6 5   5   6   6 5
     4 3   5   4 3

(2)

Publifh, fpread to All around,
The great Immanuel's Name,
Let the Trumpet's martial Sound,
Him Lord of Host proclaim:
Praise Him ev'ry tuneful String,
All the Reach of heav'nly Art,
All the Powers of Music bring,
The Music of the Heart.

(3)

Him, in whom they move, and live,
Let every Creature sing,
Glory to their Maker give,
And Homage to their King:
Hallow'd be his Name beneath,
As in Heaven on Earth ador'd,
Praise the Lord in every Breath;
Let all Things praise the Lord.

Cirencester

Praise ye the Lord y'immortal Choir, That fill the Realms a-

y'immortal Choir, That fill the Realms a-

bove; Praise Him who form'd you of his Fire, And feeds you &

bove; Praise Him who form'd you of his Fire, &

feeds you with his Love: Shine to his Praise, ye crystal

feeds you with his Love: Shine to his Praise, ye crystal

Skies, the Floor of his a _ _ bode Or veil in Shades

Skies, the Floor of his a _ _ _ bode

your Thousand Eyes, Be _ fore   be _ fore your brighter God.

your Thousand Eyes, Be _ fore   be _ fore yourbrighter God.

2

Thou restless Globe of golden Light,
 Whose Beams create our Day,
Join with the Silver Queen of Night.
 To own your borrow'd Rays:
Winds, ye shall bear his Name aloud,
 Thro' the etherial Blue;
For when his Chariot is a Cloud,
 He makes his Wheels of you.

3

Thunder and Hail and Fire and Storms,
 The Troops of his Command,
Appear in all your dreadful Forms,
 And speak his awful Hand:
Shout to the Lord, ye furging Seas
 In your eternal Roar;
Let Wave to Wave resound his Praise,
 And Shore reply to Shore.

4

Wave your tall Heads, ye lofty Pines,
 To him that bids you grow;
Sweet Clusters bend the fruitful Vines,
 On ev'ry thankful Bough:
Thus while the meaner Creatures fing,
 Ye Mortals, take the Sound:
Echo the Glories of your King,
 Thro' all the Nation round:

Bedford

Set by W. B.

Meet and right it is to sing Glory to our

Meet and right it is to sing Glory to our

God and King: Meet in ev_ry Time and Place,

God and King: Meet in ev_ry Time and Place,

To re hearse his so__lemn Praise. Meet in ev_ry

To re hearse his so__lemn Praise. Meet in ev_ry

Time and Place,   To re _ _hearse his folemn Praise

Time and Place,   To re _ _hearse his folemn Praise

2

Join, ye Saints, the Song around,
Angels help the chearful Sound;
Publish thro' the World abroad
Glory to th' eternal God.

3

Praises here to Thee we give,
Gracious Thou our Thanks receive;
Holy Father, Sov'reign Lord,
Ev'ry where be Thou ador'd!

4

Tho' th' injurious World exclaim,
Sing we ftill in Jefu's Name;
Saviour, Thee we ever blefs,
Thee our Lord and God confefs.

Leicester.

Set by M.M.

Sweet is the Work, O God, our King To praise thy

Sweet is the Work, O God, our King To praise thy

5 6 6

Name, give Thanks, and fing To shew thy Love by Morning

Name, give Thanks, and fing To shew thy Love by Morning

6 6 6
4

Light, And talk of all thy Truth by Night. Sweet

Light, And talk of all thy Truth by Night. Sweet

is the Day of Sa _ cred Rest, No mor _ _ tal Care shall

is the Day of Sa _ cred Rest, no mortal Care shall

feize our Breast. O may our Hearts in Tune be

feize our Breast. O may our Hearts in Tune be

found, Like Da--vid's Harp, of folemn Sound.

found, Like Da--vid's Harp, of folemn Sound.

2

Our Hearts fhould triumph in Thee, Lord,
And blefs thy Works, and blefs thy Word;
Thy Works of Grace, how bright they fhine.
How deep thy Counfels! how divine!
O may we fee, and hear, and know,
What Mortals cannot reach below:
May all our Pow'rs find fweet Employ
In Chrift's eternal World of Joy!

The Pilgrim's Song

Set by I. W.

Rise, my Soul, and stretch thy Wings, Thy better Portion trace:

Rise, my Soul, and stretch thy Wings, Thy better Portion trace:

Rise from tran-si - to - ry Things, Tow'rds Heav'n . . . Tow'rds

Rise from tran-si - to - ry Things, Tow'rds Heav'n . . . Tow'rds

Heav'n thy na - tive Place. - - - Tow'rds Heav'n thy native Place,

Heav'n thy na - tive Place. - - Tow'rds Heav'n thy native Place,

- - - Sun, and Moon, and Stars de - - cay, Time shall soon this

- - - Sun, and Moon, and Stars de - - cay, Time shall soon this

Earth re-move; Rise, my Soul, and haste a--way, To Seats pre-

Earth re-move; Rise, my Soul, and haste a--way, To Seats pre-

-par'd a--bove.... To Seats pre-par'd a bove.

-par'd a--bove.... To Seats pre-par'd a bove.

(2)

Rivers to the Ocean run,
Nor stay in all their Course:
Fire ascending seeks the Sun,
Both speed them to their Source:

(3)

So a Soul that's born of God.
Pants to view his glorious Face,
Upwards tends to his Abode,
To rest in his Embrace.

(4)

Cease, ye Pilgrims, cease to mourn,
Press onward to the Prize:
Soon our Saviour will return,
Triumphant in the Skies:

(5)

Yet a Season and you know
Happy Entrance will be given,
All our Sorrows left below,
And Earth exchang'd for Heav'n.

120 **Mansfield** Set by C.B.

Awake our Souls (away our Fears, let ev'ry trembling

Awake our Souls (away our Fears, let ev'ry trembling

Awake our Souls (away our Fears, let ev'ry trembling

Thought be gone) A--wake and run the heav'nly

Thought be gone) A--wake and run the heav'nly

Thought be gone) A--wake and run the

Race, And put a chear-ful Cour-age on And

Race, And put a chear-ful Cour-age on And

heav'n-ly Race, and put a chear-ful Cour-age on And

put a chear...ful Cour...age on.

put a chear...ful Cour...age on.

put a chear...ful Cour...age on.

2

True 'tis a strait and thorny Road,
And mortal Spirits' tire and faint:
But we forget the mighty God,
That feeds the Strength of ev'ry Saint.

3

O mighty God, thy matchlefs Pow'r
Is ever new and ever young:
And firm endures, while endlefs Years
This everlasting Circles run.

4

From Thee, the overflowing Spring,
Believers drink a fresh Supply,
While, such as trust their native Strength,
Shall fade away, and droop, and die.

5

Swift as an Eagle cuts the Air,
Oh may we mount to thine Abode,
On Wings of Love, to Jesus fly,
Nor tire amidst the heav'nly Road.

Hartford.

Set by T. H.

The Lord fup..plies his Peo...ple's Need,

The Lord fup...plies his Peo...ple's Need,

Je...ho...vah is his Name; In Pas..tures

Je...ho...vah is his Name; In Pas..tures

fresh he makes them feed, Be_side the liv___ing

fresh he makes them feed, Be_side the liv_..ing

Stream, Be - side the liv - - - ing Stream.

Stream. Be - side the liv - - - ing Stream.

2

He brings their wand'ring Spirits back,
  When they forsake his Ways,
And leads them, for his Mercy's Sake,
  In Paths of Truth and Grace.

3

When they walk thro' the Shades of Death,
  His Presence is their Stay:
A Word of his supporting Breath
  Drives all their Fears away.

4

His Hand in Sight of all their Foes
  Doth still their Table spread,
Their Cup with Blessings overflows,
  His Oil anoints their Head.

5

The sure Provisions of our God,
  Attend us all our Days
O may his House be our Abode,
  And all our Work his Praise.

Pewsey

Set by M.M.

Thou Je_ _sus art our King. Thy ceaseless Praise we

Thou Je_ _sus art our King. Thy ceaseless Praise we

fing; Praise shall our glad Tongue em_ploy; Praise o'er_

fing; Praise shall our glad Tongue em_ploy. Praise o'er_

_ flow our grateful Soul, While we vi_ _tal Breath en_

_ flow our grateful Soul, While we vi_ _tal Breath en_

2
Thou art th' eternal Light,
That shin'st in deepest Night,
Wond'ring gaz'd th' angelic Train
While Thou bow'dst the Heav'ns beneath;
God with God wert Man with Man,
Man to save from endless Death.

3
Thou with our Pain didst mourn,
Thou hast our Sickness born:
All our Sins on Thee were laid!
Thou with unexampled Grace
All the mighty Debt hast paid,
Due from Adam's helpless Race.

4
Enthron'd above yon Sky,
Thou reign'st with God most high:
Prostrate at thy Feet we fall!
Pow'r supreme to Thee is given,
Thee, the righteous Judge of all,
Thee, the Lord of Earth and Heav'n!

5
Arise! stir up thy Pow'r,
Thou deathless Conqueror!
King of all, with pitying Eye
Mark the Toil, the Pains we feel!
'Midst the Snares of Death we lie,
'Midst the banded Pow'rs of Hell.

6
O Lord! O God of Love!
Let us thy Mercy prove!
Help us to obtain the Prize,
Help us well to close our Race;
That with Thee, above the Skies,
Endless Joy we may possess.

Denbigh

Set by M.M.

From all that dwell be_low the Skies, Let the Cre___a__tor's

From all that dwell be_low the Skies, Let the Cre___a__tor's

Praise a_rise; Let the Re_deemer's Name be sung, thro' e__v'ry

Praise a_rise; Let the Re_deemer's Name be sung, thro' ev'ry

Land by e_v'ry Tongue. E__ter_nal are thy Mercies, Lord, E_

Land by e__v'ry Tongue. E__ter_nal are thy Mercies, Lord, E_

-ter-nal Truth at-tends thy Word; Thy Praise shall sound from
-ter-nal Truth at-tends thy Word; Thy Praise shall sound from
Shore to Shore, Till Suns shall rise and set no more. Till
Shore to Shore, Suns shall rise and set no more. Till
Suns shall rise and set no more. Till Suns shall rise and set no more.
Suns shall rise and set no more. Till Suns shall rise and set no more.
p
pp
p. dim.
f.
tr

Lambeth

Set by C.B.

Long have we sat beneath the Sound Of thy Sal-

Long have we sat beneath the Sound Of thy Sal-

-va--tion, Lord, But still how weak our Faith is found, And

--va--tion, Lord, But still how weak our Faith is found, And

Knowledge of thy Word! Oft we fre--

Knowledge of thy Word! Oft we fre--

-quent thine ho - - ly Place, Yet hear al - most in vain Sy
-quent thine ho - - ly Place, Yet hear al - most in vain Sy
How small a Por - - tion of thy Grace Do
How small a Por - - tion of thy Grace Do
our false Hearts re - tain! How fmall a Por - - tion
our false Hearts re - tain! How fmall a Por - - tion
of thy Grace Do our false Hearts re - tain.
of thy Grace Do our false Hearts re - tain.

3

Our gracious Saviour and our God
How little art Thou known,
In all the Judgments of thy Rod,
And Bleffings of Thy Throne.

4

How cold and feeble is our Love,
How negligent our Fears!
How low our Hope of Joys above.
How few Affections there!

5

Great God, thy sov'reign Aid impart,
To give thy Word Success;
Write thy Salvation on our Heart,
And makes us learn thy Grace.

6

Show our forgetful Feet the Way,
That leads to Joys on high;
Where Knowledge grows without Decay.
And Love shall never die.

Dunstan.

Set by M. M.

Glory and Honour be to Thee, Thou felf ex-is--tent De--i--ty; Thee we re---vere, and

2

To Thee, our joyful Hearts we raise,
To Thee, we bring our Songs of Praise.
Whose bounteous Care and Love imparts
Celestial Blefsings to our Hearts.

3

Unto the holy Tribune God,
Who hast on us, poor Worms, bestow'd
Such Favours, such amazing Grace,
We pay our Homage, Thanks and Praise.

Kingston.

Set by M.M.

Hail holy holy holy Lord! Be endless Praise Praise to
Thee! Supreme essential One adored In co-e-ternal Three! Enthron'd in ever lasting State, e'er
Time its round began, Who join'd in Council to create the

Dig - ni - - ty of Man. The Dig - ni - - ty of Man.

Dig - ni - - ty of Man. The Dig - ni - - ty of Man.

3

To whom Isaiah's Vision shew'd,
 The Seraphs veil their Wings,
While Thee Jehovah, Lord, and God,
 Th'angelic Army sing.

4

To Thee by mystic Pow'rs on high
 Were humble Praises given,
When John beheld with favour'd Eye
 Th' Inhabitants of Heaven.

5

All that the Name of Creature owns,
 To Thee in Hymns aspire;
May we as Angels on our Thrones
 For ever join the Choir!

6

Hail holy, holy holy Lord!
 Be endless Praise to Thee;
Supreme, essential One, ador'd
 In co-eternal Three.

Norwich

Set by I.W.

Andante

To Fa — ther, Son, and Ho — ly

To Fa — ther, Son, and Ho — ly

Ghost, Be Praise a — midst the heav'n — ly

Ghost, Be Praise a — midst the heav'n — ly

Host, And in the Church be — low From whom all

Host, And in the Church be — low From whom all

Crea-tures drew their Birth, By whom Re-demption blest the

Crea-tures drew their Birth, By whom Re-demption blest the

Earth, From whom all Com-forts flow. From

Earth, From whom all Com-forts flow. From

whom all Com-----forts flow.

whom all Com-----forts flow.

Stratham.

136

Set by C. L.

Blest are the Souls that hear and know The Gof _ pel's

Blest _ are the Souls that hear and know The Gof _ pel's

joy _ ful Sound   The Gospel's joy _ full Sound.

joy _ ful Sound   The Gospel's joy _ full Sound.

Peace shall at _ _ tend the Path they

Peace shall at _ _ tend the Path they

go, And Light their Steps sur _ round.

go, And Light their Steps sur _ round.

Peace fhall at.tend the Path they go, And Light their Steps sur.

Peace fhall at.tend the Path they go, And Light their Steps sur.

6 6/4 6 6/4 7

_ _ round.   And Light   their Steps sur _ round.

_ _ round.   And Light   their Steps sur_ round.

6   6   6 6/4   6   6/4 5/3

2

Their Joy fhall bear their Spirits up,
Thro' their Redeemer's Name;
His Righteousness exalts their Hope,
Nor Satan dares condemn.
The Lord our Glory and Defence,
Strength and Salvation gives:
Israel, thy King for ever reigns.
Thy God for_ever lives .

LOCK HOSPITAL

A New

AND

IMPROVED EDITION OF

The Collection of

PSALM & HYMN TUNES,

SUNG

at the CHAPEL of the

LOCK HOSPITAL.

Book 3

Price 5

London

Printed by Broderip & Wilkinson, 13 Hay-market

Where are Printed. the 1st 2nd 3rd & 4th. Books of the Magdalen Hymns. 2s each

INDEX

Book. III.

Nantwich.

Set by M.M.

Andante

O God, how end_less is thy Love! Thy

O God, how end_less is thy Love! Thy

6   6 5
         4 3

Gifts are ev'_ry Ev'ning new; And Morn_ing

Gifts are ev'_ry Ev'ning new; And Morn_ing

6

Mercies from a__bove, Gent__ly dis__till like

Mercies from a__bove, Gent__ly dis__till like

9   5   6   5   6   6 5   6 5 6
1   3

ear _ _ ly Dew. Gent_ly dis _ _ till like ear_ly Dew.

ear _ _ ly Dew. Gent_ly dis _ _ till like ear_ly Dew.

(2)

Thou spread'st the Curtain of the Night,
Great Guardian of our sleeping Hours;
Thy Sov'reign Word restores the Light,
And quickens all our drowsy Pow'rs.

(3)

We yield our Pow'rs to thy Command,
To Thee we consecrate our Days,
Perpetual Blessings from thine Hand,
Demand perpetual Songs of Praise.

Lothbury

Sa - viour   Sa - viour   Sa - viour and

Sa - viour   Sa - viour and

can it be, That Thou shouldst dwell with me!

can it be, That Thou shouldst dwell with me!

From thine high and lof - - ty Throne,   Throne of

From thine high and lof - - ty Throne,   Throne of

e - - ver last - ing Bliss.   Will thy

e - - ver last - ing Bliss.   Will thy

Majesty thy Majesty stoop down.   To so mean an

Majesty thy Majesty stoop down.   To so mean an

House as this.   Will thy Majesty thy

House as this.   Will thy Majesty thy

Majesty stoop down. . . . s. mean an House as this.

Majesty steep down. . . . s. . . an an House as this.

I am not worthy, Lord,
So foul, and self-abhorr'd,
Thee, my God, to entertain,
In this poor polluted Heart;
I am a frail sinful Man,
All my Nature cries Depart.

Yet come! thou Heav'nly Guest,
And purify my Breast!
Come! thou great and glorious King,
While before thy Cross I bow
With Thyself Salvation bring,
Cleanse the House by ent'ring now.

Gloria Patri

Set by M. M.

Sing we to our God above, Praise eternal as His.

Sing we to our God above, Praise eternal as His

Love: Praise Him all ye heav'nly Host Father, Son and

Love: Praise Him all ye heav'nly Host Father, Son and

Holy Ghost. Praise Him, all ye heav'nly Host, Father,

Holy Ghost. Praise Him, all ye heav'nly Host, Father,

Son, and Holy Ghost.

Bredby.

Vivace

Now to the Pow'r of God Su _ preme Be e _ _ ver _

Now to the Pow'r of God Su _ preme Be e _ _ ver _

6   6   6

_ las _ ting e _ _ ver las _ ting Honour giv'n He saves from

_ las _ ting e _ _ ver las _ ting Honour giv'n He saves from

6   6   6 5   6
              4   3

Hell, (we bless his Name) He calls lost wand' _ ring

Hell, (we bless his Name) He calls lost wand' _ ring

                              6   7   6
                              4

Soul to Heav'n, He calls lost wand'ring Souls to Heav'n

Soul to Heav'n, He calls lost wand'ring Souls to Heav'n

2

Not for our Duties or Deserts
But of his own abounding Grace,
He works Salvation in our Hearts,
And forms a People for his Praise.

3

'Twas his own Purpose that begun
To rescue Rebels doom'd to die,
He gave us Grace in Christ his Son,
Before he spread the starry Sky.

4

Jesus, the Lord, appears at last,
And makes his Father's Councils known,
Declares the greate Transaction's past,
And brings immortal Blessings down.

Easter.

Set by M. M.

Andante Affettuoso

He dies the Friend of Sin _ ners dies. Lo!

He dies the Friend of Sin _ ners dies. Lo!

Salem's Daughters weep a round a fo_lemn Darkncfs

Salem's Daughters weep a round a fo_lemn Darknefs

veils the Skies, a fud_den Trembling fhakes the Ground.

veils the Skies, a fud_den Trembling fhakes the Ground.

tutti p.

ada. ad lib.

Come Saints and drop a Tear or two for

organo

Come Saints and drop a Tear or two for

Him who groan'd beneath your Load, He shed a thousand drops for you a

Him who ground beneath your Load, He shed a thousand drops for you a

thousand drops of richer Blood.

thousand drops of richer Blood.

Affettuoso

Here's Love and Grief beyond Degree, the Lord of Glory dies for Men. But lo! what sudden Joys we feel! Jesus the Dead revives again.

Vivace

The rising God for - sakes the Tomb, in vain the Tomb for

The rising God for - sakes the Tomb, in vain the Tomb for

bids his Rise! Che - ru-bic Le-gions guard Him home, and

bids his Rise! Che - ru-bic Le-gions guard Him home, and

shout Him wel - come to the Skies.

shout Him wel - come to the Skies.

Vivace
Break off your Tears ye Saints! and tell how
Break off your Tears ye Saints! and tell how
high our great De - - liv'rer reigns
2 time. forte
Sing how He
high our great De - - liv'rer reigns Sing how He
Octaves
fpoil'd the Hosts of Hell, and led the Mon - ster
fpoil'd the Hosts of Hell, and led the Mon - ster
Death in Chains! Say Live for ever, wond'rous
Death in Chains! Say Live for ever, wond'rous

King! Born to re_deem! and ftrong to save, Then

King! Born to re_deem! and ftrong to save, Then

6 5   5   7   — 43 6 5
4 5   5   4 3

ask the Monster where's thy , Sting? And

ask the Monster where's thy Sting? And

4 6   6   6 6 7 — 5
2

where's thy Vic_to_ry boast__ing Grave? And

where's thy Vic_to_ry boast__ing Grave? And

6   6   6 5 6 5
           4 3 4 3

where's thy Vic_to_ry boast___ing Grave?

where's thy Vic_to_ry boast___ing Grave?

5 7 5   6   9 8 6 5
             7 6 4 3

Roehampton

Set by C.L.

Rise your triumphant Songs   To an immortal

Rise your triumphant Songs   To an immortal

6   6   9 8   6 5
          7 6   4 ♯3

Tune   Let the wide Earth re-sound the Deeds Ce-

Tune   Let the wide Earth re-sound the Deeds Ce-

4   5   6   5   6   6   6
2   3   4   3

-les-tial Grace has done, Ce-les-tial   Grace has done Sing

-les-tial Grace has done, Ce-les-tial   Grace has done Sing

6   6   6   6   6   6   4 3
     7   4   4
              5
              3

how e--ter-nal Love Its chief Be-lo-ved

how e--ter-nal Love Its chief Be-lo-ved

chose, and bid Him raise our wretched Race from

chose, and bid Him raise our wretched Race from

their A-byfs of Woes, and bid Him raise our wretched Race from

their A-byfs of Woes, and bid Him raise our wretched Race from their A_byss of Woes. from their A_byss of Woes

their A_byss of Woes. from their A_byss of Woes

3

His Hand no Thunder bears,
No Terror cloaths his Brow;
No Bolts to drive our guilty Souls
To fiercer Flames below.

4

'Twas Mercy fill'd the Throne,
And Wrath stood silent by,
When Christ was sent with Pardons down
To Rebels doom'd to die.

Sym:

Now Now

Now Now

Sin _ ners dry your Tears,   Let hopeless

Sin _ ners dry your Tears,   Let hopeless

hopeless Sorrows cease;   Bow to the

hopeless Sorrows cease;   Bow to the

Sceptre   of his Love, and take the of _ fer'd   Peace.

Sceptre   of his Love, and take the of _ fer'd   Peace.

ff
Bow to the Sceptre of his Love, and take the of-fer'd
Bow to the Sceptre of his Love, and take the of-fer'd
Peace. May we o - - bey the Call! Sy And
Peace. May we o - - bey the Call! And
lay an hum - - ble Claim. To the Sal-
tr
Sym.
lay an hum - - ble Claim. To the Sal-

-- va - tion He hath brought, and love and praise his
-- va - tion He hath brought, and love and praise his
Name! To the Sal - va - - tion He hath brought, and love and
Name! To the Sal - va - - tion He hath brought, and love and
praise his Name! and love and praise his Name!
praise his Name! and love and praise his Name!

Colchefter.

Set by M.M.

Th'extent of Jefu's Love What Heart can compre-hend. A

Th'extent of Jefu's Love What Heart can compre-hend. A

Breadth whose Distance none can prove, A Length without an

Breadth whose Distance none can prove, A Length without an

End. The first born Seraphs try the Myst'ry to explore, they

End. The first born Seraphs try the Myst'ry to explore, they

can not find it out, for why, The Curse they ne-ver bore The

can not find it out, for why, The Curse they ne-ver bore The

Curse they never bore.

Curse they never bore.

(2)

The Grace unsearchable,
Transcending human Thought,
Who, who, in Earth or Heav'n can tell,
Or find the Wonder out!
All the Angelic Choir
Unite to give Him Praise;
And Saints redeeming Love admire,
And loud Hosannahs raise.

(3)

To Christ we list our Voice,
Who have Redemption found·
And in His Name alone rejoice,
Whence all our Joys abound,
This cures the burden'd Mind,
This calms the troubled Heart;
This manifests the Saviour Kind,
And bids our Fears depart.

Deptford.

Father, Son, and Ho_ly Ghost, One in Three, and

Father, Son, and Ho_ly Ghost, One in Three, and

Three in One as by the Ce_lestial Host Let thy

Three in One as by the Ce_lestial Host Let thy

will on Earth be done, Let thy will on

will on Earth be done. Let thy will on

Earth be done   Praise by all to Thee be given

Earth be done   Praise by all to Thee be given

Glo_rious Lord of Earth and Heav'n. Glo_rious Lord of

Glo_rious Lord of Earth and Heav'n. Glo_rious Lord of

Earth and Heav'n Praise by all to Thee be given.

Earth and Heav'n Praise by all to Thee be given.

Glorious Lord of Earth and Heav'n.

Glorious Lord of Earth and Heav'n.

2

If so poor a Worm as I,
May to thy great Glory live,
All mine Actions sanctify,
All my Thoughts and Words receive.
Claim me for thy Service — claim
All I have, and all I am.

3

Take my Soul and Body's Pow'rs,
Take my Mem'ry Mind and Will,
All my Goods, and all mine Hours,
All I know, and all I feel,
All I think, and speak, and do,
Take mine Heart — but not eitnew.

4

Father, Son, and Holy Ghost,
One in Three, and Three in One,
As by the Cœlestial Host.
Let thy Will on Earth be done!
Praise by all to Thee be giv'n,
Glorious Lord of Earth and Heav'n.

Buckingham

Set by C. L.

Praise be to the Fa_ther gi_ven Christ He gave

Praise be to the Fa_ther gi_ven Christ He gave

us to fave, Now the Heirs the Heirs of Heaven

us to fave, Now the Heirs the Heirs of Heaven

Now the Heirs the Heirs of Heaven.

Now the Heirs the Heirs of Heaven.

2

Pay we equal Adoration
To the Son
He alone
Wrought out our Salvation.

3

Glory to th'Eternal Spirit,
Us He seals,
Christ reveals
And applies his Merit.

4

Worship, Honour, Thanks and Blessing,
One in Three,
Give we Thee,
Never, never ceasing.

Clapham.

Set by C. L.

Let Earth and Heav'n a - - gree. Sy

Let Earth and Heav'n a - - gree.

6   9 8 6 5
            7 6 4 3

An-gels and Men be join'd Sy To.

An-gels and Men be join'd To

6   7   6 5
          4 3

ce - le - - brate with me - - - - - The

ce - - le - - brate with me - - - - - The

8#7 6#7   6 5   7   7#3
     4 2   4 3   #

Sa__viour of Man kind; The Sa__viour

Sa__viour of Man kind; The Sa__viour

of Man _ kind. T'a __ dore the all a __

of Man _ kind. T'a __ dore the all a __

_ to __ ning Lamb, And blefs the Sound of

_ to __ ning Lamb, And blefs the Sound of

Je _ _ su's Name   T'a _

Je _ _ su's Name   T'a _

_ _ dore the   all a _ _ _ to _ ning Lamb, and blefs the

_ _ dore the   all a _ _ _ to _ ning Lamb, and blefs the

Sound   of   Je _ _ fu's   Name.   Sy

Sound   of   Je _ _ fu's   Name.

And blefs the Sound of Je-su's Name.

And blefs the Sound of Je-su's Name.

(2)

Jefus! transporting Sound;
  The Joy of Earth and Heav'n!
No other Help is found,
  No other Name is giv'n,
By which we can Salvation have —
But Jesus came the World to fave.

(3)

Jefus! harmonious Name!
  It charms the Hofts above!
They evermore proclaim,
  And wonder at his Love!
'Tis all their Happinefs to gaze,
'Tis Heav'n to fee, our Jefu's Face.

(4)

His Name Sinner hears,
  And is from Sin fet free;
'Tis Mufic in his Ears,
  'Tis Life and Victory:
New Songs do now his Lips employ,
And dances his glad Heart for Joy.

Tadcaster

Set by C.L.

Come thou Fount of e - v - ry Blefsing,

Come thou Fount of e - v - ry Blefsing,

7

Tune mine Heart to sing thy Grace. Tune mine

Tune mine Heart to sing thy Grace. Tune mine

Heart to sing thy Grace. Streams of Mer - cy

Heart to sing thy Grace. Streams of Mer - cy

ne _ _ ver ceasing Call for Songs of loud _ _ est

ne _ _ ver ceasing Call for Songs of loud _ _ est

5 6 6   6 5   6   6 6 6
                                        4

Praise, Call for Songs of loud _ _ _ est

Praise, Call for Songs of loud _ _ _ est

6   7   5   6   6   5
                                      4   3

Praise, Teach me fome me _ _ lo _ dious Son _ net,

Praise, Teach me fome me _ _ lo _ dious Son _ net,

6   6   #6   6   5
                  4   5   #

Sung by flam-ing Tongues a--bove.

Sung by flam-ing Tongues a--bove.

Praise the Mount I'm fix'd up-on it

Praise the Mount I'm fix'd up-on it

Mount of Gods un-chang-ing Love. Mount of

Mount of Gods un-chang-ing Love. Mount of

Gods un_ chang _ _ing Love.

Gods un_ chang _ _ ing Love.

2

Here I raise my Eben_ezer,
Hither by thine Help I'm come;
And I hope, by thy good Pleasure,
Safely to arrive at Home:
Jesus sought me, when a Stranger,
Wand'ring from the Fold of God.
He, to rescue me from Danger,
Interpos'd with precious Blood.

3

O! to Grace, how great a Debtor,
Daily I'm constrain'd to be!
Let that Grace now, like a Fetter,
Bind my wand'ring Heart to Thee!
Prone to wander, Lord, I feel it.
Prone to leave the God I Love—
Here's mine Heart—O take, and seal it!
Seal it from thy Courts above!

Harborough

Set by C. B.

Vivace Chorus

Lift up your Heads in joy _ _ ful Hope, Sa _ _ lute the

Lift up your Heads in joy _ _ ful Hope, Sa _ _ lute the

hap _ py the hap _ _ py Morn; each Heav'nly Pow'r, pro_

hap _ py the hap _ _ py Morn; each Heav'nly Pow'r, pro_

_ claims the glad Hour, Lo Je_ fus the Saviour is born! Lo

_ claims the glad Hour, Lo Je_ fus the Saviour is born! Lo

Je _ fus the Sa _ _ _ _ _ viour is born!

Je _ fus the Sa _ _ _ _ viour is born!

All Glory to God on high,
To Him all Praife is due;
The Promife is feal'd,
The Saviour's reveal'd,
And proves that the Record is true.

Grazioso e Pia.

Let Joy around like Rivers flow, flow on, and

Let Joy around like Rivers flow, flow on and

ftill in creafe; Spread o'er the glad Earth at Je fus his Birth for

ftill in creafe; Spread o'er the glad Earth at Je fus his Birth for

Heav'n and Earth are at Peace. for Heav'n and Earth are at
Heav'n and Earth are at Peace. for Heav'n and Earth are at
6 6 4 5 3 7 6 4 5 3
Peace. Now the Good will of Heav'n is shewn tow'rds Adam's
Peace. Now the Good will of Heav'n is shewn tow'rds Adam's
6 4 6 4 5
helplefs help- -lefs Race; Mef- -fi- -ah is come to
helplefs help- -lefs Race; Mef- -fi- -ah is come to
6 3 6 5 6 4

ransom his Own, To fave them to fave them by In-fi-nite Grace. To

ransom his Own, To fave fave them by In-fi-nite Grace. To

fave to fave them by In-fi-nite Grace.

First Chorus

Then let us

fave to fave them by In-fi-nite Grace.

Then let us

tutti

join the Heav'ns a - - bove.

join the Heav'ns a - - bove.

Then let us join the Heav'ns above
Where hymning Seraphs sing,
Join all the glad Pow'rs,
For their Lord is Ours.
Our Prophet, our Priest, and our King.

The Nativity.

Set by C.B.

Hark! Hark! Herald Angels fing, Glo - ry

Hark! Hark! Herald Angels fing, Glo - ry

Soli pia

to the new born King! Peace on Earth and

to the new born King! Peace on Earth and

tutti for.   Org:

Mer - cy mild God and Sin - ners re - con - cil'd

Mer - cy mild God and Sin - ners re - con - cil'd

Joyful all ye

Joyful all ye

$$\frac{6}{4} \quad \frac{5}{\natural 3}$$

$\natural 3$

Na _ _ tions rise. Join the Triumphs of the

Na _ _ tions rise. Join the Triumphs of the

$6 \quad \#3 \qquad \frac{6}{4} - \frac{5}{3}$

Skies. With th'an _ _ ge _ _ lic Hoft pro _ _ claim.

Skies. With th'an _ _ ge _ _ lic Hoft pro _ _ claim.

$$\frac{7}{5} \; \frac{6}{4} - \frac{7}{5} \qquad 6 \qquad \frac{6}{4} \; \frac{5}{3}$$

Chrift is born in Beth-le--hem. Chrift is Bo-----

Chrift is born in Beth-le--hem. Chrift is Bo-----

-----rn in Beth-le-hem. Hark! the Herald Angels

-----rn in Beth-le-hem. Hark! the Herald Angels

fing, Glo-ry to--- the new-born King.

fing, Glo-ry to the new-born King.

3

Chrift, by higheft Heav'n ador'd,
Chrift the everlafting Lord;
Late in Time behold him come,
Offs'pring of a Virgins Womb.

4

Veil'd in Flesh the Godhead fee,
Hail th' Incarnate Deity!
Pleas'd as Man with Men t'appear.
Jefus our Immanuel here.

5

Hail the Heav'n born Prince of Peace!
Hail the Sun of Rightcoufnefs!
Light and Life to all he brings,
Ris'n with Healing in his Wings.

6

Mild he lays his Glory by,
Born, that Man no more may die;
Born to raise the Sons of Earth,
Born to give them fecond Birth.

Stockwell

Set by **C.L.**

How glorious the Lamb is feen on his Throne! His

How glorious the Lamb is feen on his Throne! His

Labours are o'er His Conquests put on; A Kingdom is giv'n in-to

Labours are o'er His Conquests put on; A Kingdom is giv'n in-to

the Lamb's Hand, in Earth and in Heav'n for ever - to

the Lamb's Hand, in Earth and in Heav'n for ever- to

ftand. in Earth and in Heav'n, for e - ver to ftand.

ftand. in Earth and in Heav'n, for e - ver to ftand.

Ye Sinners below   2 Athirst for his Favour,
Then trust in the Lord,   His Godhead adore,
Look up to his Arm,   Look up to your Saviour,
His Honour, his Word: And Joy evermore.

Wickham

Set by C. B.

O Thou in whom the Gen_-tiles trust, Thou on-ly ho-ly

O Thou in whom the Gen_-tiles trust, Thou on-ly ho-ly

O Thou in whom the Gen_-tiles trust, Thou on-ly

on_-_ly juft, Oh tune our Souls to praise thy

on_-_ly juft, Oh tune our Souls to praise thy

on-ly_only juft, Oh tune our Souls to praise thy

Name, Je _ _ fus! Un _ changeable, unchange _ _ _ a _ ble the

Name, Je _ _ fus! Un _ changeable, unchange _ _ _ a _ ble the

Name, Je _ _ fus! Un _ changeable, un _ _ changeable the

Same! If An _ _ gels whilft to Thee they

Same! If An _ _ gels whilft to Thee they

Same! If An _ _ gels whilft to Thee they

fing, Wrap up their Fa _ _ ces in their Wing, How

fing, Wrap up their Fa _ _ ces in their Wing, How

fing, Wrap up their Fa _ _ ces in their Wing, How

shall we fin...ful Dust draw nigh the
great, the awe...ful De...i...ty.

(3)

Glory to Thee, auspicious Lamb!
Thou holy Lord, Thou great I am!
With all our Pow'r thy Grace we bless,
Our Joy, our Peace, our Righteousness.

(4)

Live, ever glorious Jesus! live,
Worthy all Blessings to receive!
Worthy on high enthron'd to sit.
With ev'ry Pow'r beneath thy Feet.

Islington

Set by C. L.

Blest be the Fa_ther and his Love, To whose ce_lef_tial

Blest be the Fa_ther and his Love, To whose ce_lef_tial

Source we owe. Rivers of endlefs Joys a_

Source we owe. Rivers of endlefs Joys a_

_bove And Rills of Comfort here be low. Rivers of end_lefs

_bove And Rills of Comfort here be low. Rivers of end_lefs

Joys a _ _ bove, and Rills of Com_fort here be low.

Joys a _ _ bove, and Rills of Com_fort here be low.

2

Glory to Thee, great Son of God!
Forth from thy wounded Body rolls.
A precious Stream of vital Blood,
Pardon and Life for dying Souls.

3

We give the Sacred Spirit Praise,
Who, in our Hearts of Sin and Woe,
Makes living Springs of Grace arise.
And into boundless Glory flow.

4

Thus God the Father, God the Son,
And God the Spirit, we adore,
That Sea of Life and Love unknown,
Without a Bottom or a Shore.

Launceston.

Set by W. I.

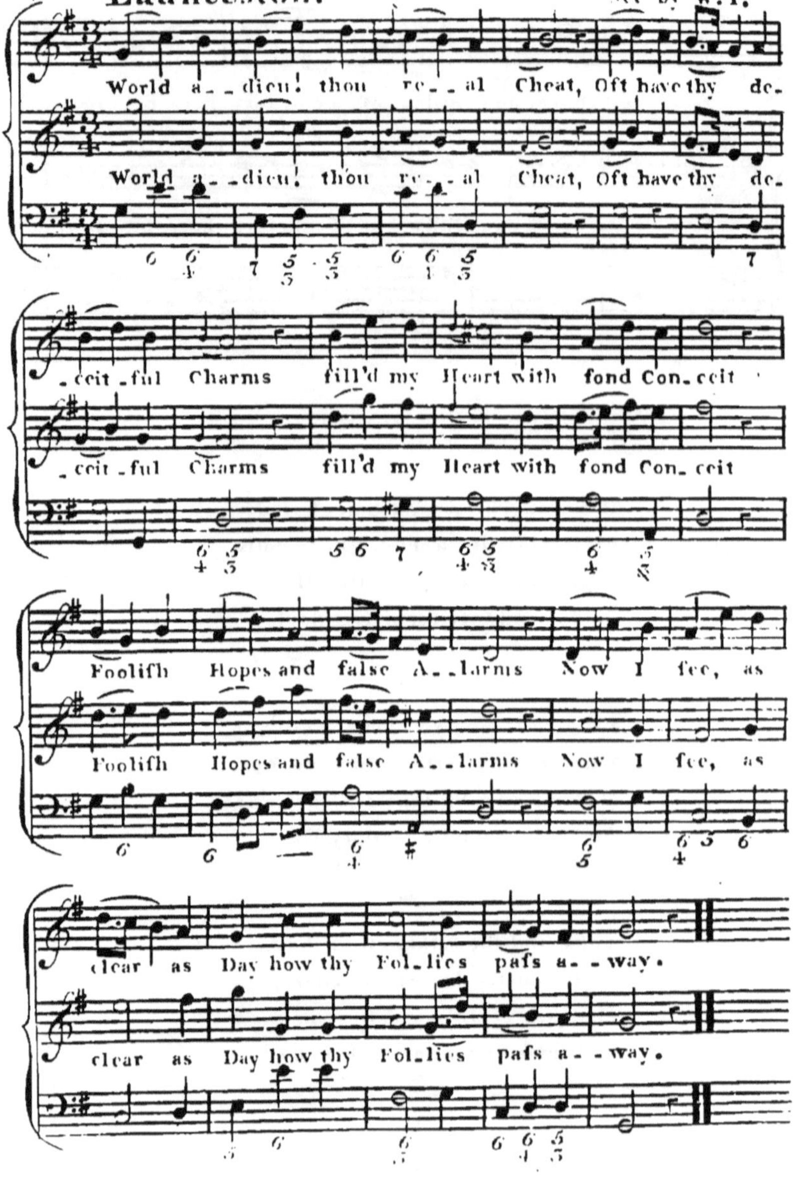

2

Vain thy entertaining Sights,
  Falfe thy Promifes renew'd,
All the Pomp of thy Delights,
  Does but flatter and delude:
Thee I quit, for Heav'n above,
  Object of the nobleft Love.

3

Farewel Honour's empty Pride,
  Thy own nice, uncertain Guft,
If the leaft Mifchance betide,
  Lays thee lower than the Dust:
Worldly Honours end in Gall,
  Rife To-day—To-morrow fall.

4

Foolifh Vanity—Farewel—
  More inconftant than the Wave,
Where thy foothing Fancies dwell,
  Pureft Tempers they deprave:
He, to whom I fly from thee,
  Jefus Chrift fhall fet me free.

5

Let not, Lord, my wand'ring Mind
  Follow after fleeting Toys,
Since, in Thee alone, I find
  Solid and fubstantial Joys:
Joys that never overpast,
  Thro' Eternity fhall last.

6

Lord! how happy is a Heart
  After Thee while it aspires!
True and faithful as Thou art,
  Thou fhalt anfwer its Desires:
It fhall see the glorious Scene
  Of thine everlasting Reign.

Denmark.

Andante Macftoso

Set by M.M.

Be _ fore Je _ _ ho _ vah's awfull Throne, Ye Na _ tions

Be _ fore Je _ ho _ vah's awfull Throne, Ye Na _ tions

bow with fa-cred Joy; Know that the Lord is God a _ _

bow with fa-cred Joy; Know that the Lord is God a _ _

_ _lone. He can cre _ _ate, and he de _ _ftroy He can cre-

_ _lone. He can cre _ _ate, and he de _ _ftroy He can cre-

_ _ate, and he de _ _ftroy. His fov'reign Pow'r, without our

_ _ate, and he de _ _ftroy. His fov'reign Pow'r, without our aid, Made us of Clay and form'd us Men; And when Like

aid, Made us of Clay and form'd us Men; And when like

wand'ring Sheep we ftray'd, He brought us to his fold a--

wand'ring Sheep we ftray'd, He brought us to his fold a--

gain. He brought us to his fold a---gain. We'll

gain. He brought us to his fold a---gain. We'll

crowd thy Gates with thank--full Songs, High as the Heav'ns our

crowd thy Gates with thank--full Songs, High as the Heav'ns our

Voi _ _ _ ces raife; And Earth, And Earth with her ten thoufand,

Voi _ _ _ ces raife; And Earth, And Earth with her ten thoufand,

thoufand Tongues Shall fill thy Courts with founding Praife Shall

thoufand Tongues Shall fill thy Courts with founding Praife Shall

fill thy Courts with founding Praife. Shall fill, fhall fill thy

fill thy Courts with founding Praife. Shall fill, fhall fill thy

Courts with found-ing Praife. Wide, wide as the World is

Courts with found-ing Praife. Wide, wide as the World is

thy Com_mand, Vast as E__ternity, E__ternity thy Love,

thy Com_mand, Vast as E__ternity, E__ternity thy Love,

Firm as a Rock thy Truth must stand When rolling Years shall

Firm as a Rock thy Truth must stand When rolling Years shall

cease to move, shall cease to move, When rolling Years shall

cease to move, shall cease to move, When rolling Years shall

cease, to move, When roll___ing Years shall cease to move.

cease, to move, When roll___ing Years shall cease to move.

Crefwick.

Set by S. A.

Come let us Join our chear_ful Songs With Angels

Chorus

Come let us Join our chear_ful Songs With Angels

Come let us Join our chear_ful Songs With Angels

round the Throne; Ten thoufand thoufand are their Tongues,but

round the Throne; Ten thoufand thoufand are their Tongues,but

round the Throne; Ten thoufand thoufand are their Tongues,but

all but all their Joys are one, ten thoufand thoufand

all but all their Joys are one, ten thoufand thoufand

all but all their Joys are one, ten thoufand thoufand

are their Tongues, but all but all their Joys are one.Ten

are their Tongues, but all but all their Joys are one.Ten

are their Tongues, but all but all their Joys are one.Ten

thousand thousand are their Tongues, but all but all their

thousand thousand are their Tongues, but all but all their

thousand thousand are their Tongues, but all but all their

Organ

Joys are one.

Joys are one.

Joys are one.

Women Duetto

Andante

Worthy the Lamb that dy'd for us, To be to be ex-

Worthy the Lamb that dy'd for us, To be to be ex-

Men Duetto _p_

_alt_ed thus: Worthy the Lamb, our Hearts reply, for he for he was

_alt_ed thus: Worthy the Lamb, our Hearts reply, for he for he was

Women.

Slain for us. Jesus is worthy to receive Honour & Pow'r &

Slain for us. Jesus is worthy to receive Honour & Pow'r &

Men.

Pow'r divine; And Blessings more than we can give, Be Lord, be

Pow'r divine; And Blessings more than we can give, Be Lord, be

Lord for e_ver thine. And Blessings more than we can give, Be Lord, be

Lord for e_ver thine. And Blessings more than we can give, Be Lord, be

Lord for e_ver thine.

Lord for e_ver thine.

Chorus.

The whole Cre-a-tion join in one, To blefs, to blefs the facred Name of

The whole Cre-a-tion join in one, To blefs, to blefs the facred Name of

him that fits up___on the Throne; And to a___

him that fits up___on the Throne; And to a___

_dore, to a-dore the Lamb. And to a__dore to a_dore the

_dore, to a-dore the Lamb. And to a_dore to a_dore the

Org:

Lamb. The whole Creation join in

Lamb. The whole Creation join in

one, to blefs to blefs the facred Name Of him that fits upon the

one, to blefs to blefs the facred Name Of him that fits upon the

Throne, And to adore to adore the Lamb. Of him that fits up.

Throne, And to adore to adore the Lamb. Of him that fits up.

6

_ on the Throne, And to a _ dore to a _ dore the Lamb. Of him that

_ on the Throne, And to a _ dore to a _ dore the Lamb. Of him that

Org:

fits up _ on the Throne, And to a _ dore to a _ dore the Lamb.

fits up _ on the Throne, And to a _ dore to a _ dore the Lamb.

The whole Cre a _ tion join in one to blefs, to

The whole Cre _ a _ tion join in one to blefs, to

bleſs the ſacred Name Of him who ſits up- on the Throne,&

bleſs the ſacred Name Of him who ſits up- on the Throne,&

to a--dore,to a-dore the Lamb.And to a--dore,to a-dore the

to a--dore,to a-dore the Lamb.And to a--dore,to a-dore the

Lamb.And to a--dore, to a- dore the Lamb.to a-dore the Lamb.

Lamb.And to a--dore, to a- dore the Lamb.to a-dore the Lamb.

Wellingborough

Larghetto

Set by I. W.

Light of those whose drea__ry dwelling

Borders __ on the Shades of Death, Come! and

by thy Love's re__veal__ing, Dis__si__

__pate the Clouds be__neath:

The new Heav'n and Earth's Cre__a__tor

In our deep-est Darkness rise!

Scatt'...ring all the Night of Na--ture

Pour-ing Eye-fight on our Eyes!

Still we wait for thine Ap-

pear-ing Life and Joy thy Beams im-part,

Chas_ing all our Fears, and chear_ing Ev'_ry

poor be__nighted Heart: Come and ma_ni_

___fest the Favour. God hath for the

ransom'd Race; Come! thou glorious God and

Saviour! Come! and bring the Gospel Grace

Larghetto

p Save us Save us in thy great Compassion,

Save us O thou mild pa_ci_fic Prince! Give the Knowledge

of Sal_va_tion Give the Pardon of our Sins! By thine

all reftoring Merit, Ev'ry burthend Soul re_lease, Ev'ry

weary wand'ring Spirit, Guide in_to thy perfect Peace!

Greenwich.

Andante   Set by M.M.

Plung'd in a Gulph of dark des_pair, We wretched,

Plung'd in a Gulph of dark des_pair, We wretched,

6 5   6 5   5 6   6
4 3   4 3

2d time for:

wretched   Sin ner   lay, With_out one chear_ful

wretched   Sin ner   lay, With_out one chear_ful

6   4 3   ♮5

Beam   of hope, Or Spark of glimm'ring Day.

Beam   of hope, Or Spark of glimm'ring Day.

7 6   6 5   6
            4 3

With pitying Eyes, the Prince of Grace Beheld our helpless, helpless Grief; He saw, and O amazing Love! He came, he came to our relief. Down from the fhining Seats a __ bove, With joyful, joy __ ful hafte he

fhining Seats a __ bove, With joyful, joy __ ful hafte he

6 5 6 5
  4 3

fled, Enter'd the Grave in mor-tal Flefh, And dwelt, and

fled, Enter'd the Grave in mor-tal Flefh, And dwelt, and

6 6 7 6 6
5

Chorus. Vivace

dwelt, and dwelt among the Dead. Oh! Oh! for this

dwelt, and dwelt among the Dead. Oh! Oh! for this

7 7 6

Love let Rocks and Hills their lasting Silence break, Their lasting

Silence break, their Silence break, And all Har-- monious

hu -- man Tongue, The Sa -- viour's Praises speak.

Chorus

Oh! Oh! for this Love let Rocks & Hills their

Oh! Oh! for this Love let Rocks & Hills their

lasting Silence break, Their lasting Silence break, their Silence break.

lasting Silence break, Their lasting Silence break, their Silence break.

Org:

Angels as‿sist our migh‿ty Joys, Strik all your

Angels as‿sist our migh‿ty Joys, Strik all your

Harps, your Harps of Gold; But when you raise your high-est

Harps, your Harps of Gold; But when you raise your high-est

Notes, your highest Notes His Love, His Love, His

Notes, your highest Notes His Love, His Love, His

Adagio ad lib:

Love can ne'er be told, His Love can ne'er be told.

Love can ne'er be told, His Love can ne'er be told.

LOCK HOSPITAL

A New

AND

IMPROVED EDITION OF

The Collection of

PSALM & HYMN TUNES,

SUNG

at the CHAPEL of the

LOCK HOSPITAL.

Book 11   Price 5

London

Printed by Broderip & Wilkinson, 13 Hay-market

Where are Printed the 1.st 2.nd 3.rd & 4.th Books of the Magdalen Hymns, 2.s each.

INDEX

BOOK IV.

Falmouth.

Set by M.M.

Lord, we come be - fore thee now, At thy feet we

Lord, we come be - fore thee now, At thy feet we

humbly bow: O do not our Suit dis - dain,

humbly bow: O do not our Suit dis - dain,

Shall we seek Thee, Lord, in vain. Lord, on Thee our

Shall we seek Thee, Lord, in vain. Lord, on Thee our

Souls de - pend, In Com - passion now de - scend:

Souls de - pend, In Com - passion now de - scend:

3

In thine own appointed Way,
Now we seek Thee here we stay;
Lord, we know not how to go
'Till a Blefsing Thou bestow.

4

Send some Message from thy word,
That may Joy and Peace afford:
Let thy Spirit now impart
Full Salvation to each Heart.

5

Comfort those who weep and mourn,
Let the time of Joy return;
Those that are cast down lift up,
Make them strong in Faith & Hope!

6

Grant that all may feek and find
Thee a God fincere and kind;
Heal the Sick, the Captive free,
Let us all rejoice in thee!

Upton

Set by S. A.

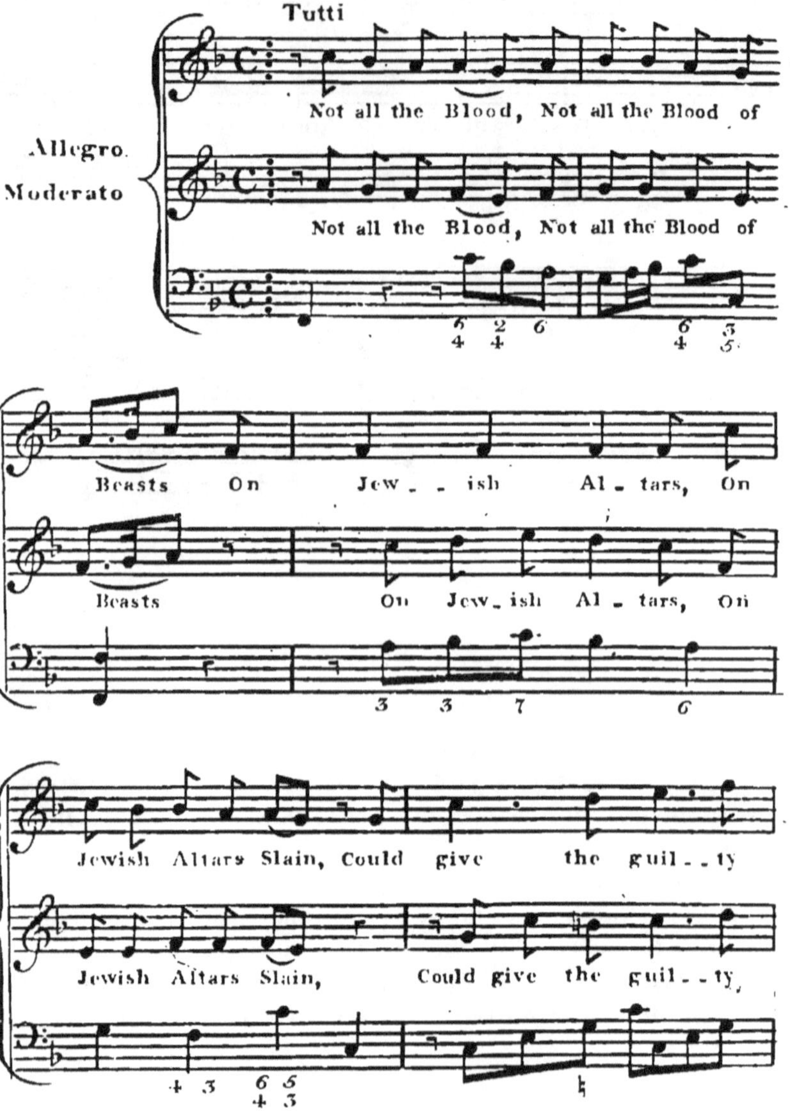

Con-science Peace, Or wash, Or wash a-

Con-science Peace, Or wash a-

1st   2d
-way the Stain.   -way the Stain. But Christ, but

-way the Stain.   -way the Stain. But Christ, but

Christ, the heav'n--ly Lamb, Takes all our Sins our

Christ, the heav'n--ly Lamb, Takes all our Sins our

Sins a _ way; A Sa _ cri _ fice of no _ _ bler

Sins a _ way; A Sa _ cri _ fice of

Name And richer rich _ _ er Blood than they

no _ bler Name, And rich _ er Blood than they

Solo

Andante My

Faith would lay it's hand On that dear head of thine,

While like a Penitent I stand And there confefs my Sin,

Organ.

My Soul looks back to fee The

Burdens thou didst bear, When hanging on th'accursed

Tree, And hopes, and hopes her Guilt was there.

Org:

Chorus. Vivace

Believing we re - - - joice to see the Curse re-

Believing we re - - - joice to see the Curse re-

move Believing we re - joice to see the Curse re-

move Believing we re - joice to see the Curse re-

move, We blefs the Lamb with chearful Voice, and

move, We blefs the Lamb with chearful Voice, and

Sing, and Sing his bleeding Love. We blefs the

Sing, and Sing his bleeding Love. We blefs the

Lamb with chearful Voice And Sing, and

Lamb with chearful Voice And Sing, and

Sing his bleed_ing Love. Be_liev-ing we re-

Sing his bleed_ing Love. Be_liev-ing we re-

-joice To see the Curse re- move; Believing we re-

-joice To see the Curse re- move; Believing we re-

joice To see the Curse re- move; We blefs the

joice To see the Curse re- move; We blefs the

Lamb with chearful Voice And Sing, and

Lamb with chearful Voice And Sing, and

Sing his bleeding Love. We blest the Lamb with

Sing his bleeding Love. We blest the Lamb with

chearful Voice and Sing, and Sing his bleeding

chearful Voice and Sing, and Sing his bleeding

Adagio

Love. his bleeding Love.

Love. his bleeding Love.

Adagio

Sussex

Set by W.M.

Our Shepherd a lone the Lord let us blefs, Who reigns on the

the Lord let us blefs, Who reigns on the

Throne the Prince of our Peace. Who evermore saves us by

Throne the Prince of our Peace. Who evermore saves us by

fhedding his Blood. All hail, all hail, holy Jesus, Our Lord and our God! All

fhedding his Blood. All hail, all hail, holy Jesus, Our Lord and our God!

hail, all hail, all hail, holy Je _ sus Our Lord and our God.

all hail, holy Je _ sus Our Lord and our God.

6 6 5 6 5
4 3

We daily will sing | Thy Kindness for ever | Preserve us in Love
Thy Merits, thy Praise, | To Men we will tell. | While here we abide;
Thou merciful Spring | And say, our dear Saviour | Nor ever remove,
Of Pity and Grace: | Redeems us from Hell. | Nor cover, nor hide.

Thy glorious Sal_vation, Till joyful we see the beautiful

Thy glorious Sal_vation, Till joyful we see the beautiful

6 5 6 5 6 6
4 3 3

Vi _ _ sion Com _ pleated in Thee.

Vi _ _ sion Com _ pleated in Thee.

7 6 6 5
4 3

Cambridge. Adagio maestoso   Set by F.G.

Fa__ther   Fa__ther, how wide thy Glo_ry fhines!

Fa__ther   Fa__ther, how wide thy Glo_ry fhines!

Fa__ther   Fa__ther, how wide thy Glo_ry fhines!

How high thy Wonders   rise!   Known thro' § Earth by

How high thy Wonders   rise!   Known thro' § Earth by

How high thy Wonders   rise!   Known thro' § Earth by

thousand Signs, By thousand thro' the Skies. Those mighty

thousand Signs, By thousand thro' the Skies. Those mighty

thousand Signs, By thousand thro' the Skies. Those mighty

Orbs proclaim thy Pow'r, Those Motions speak thy Skill.

Orbs proclaim thy Pow'r, Those Motions speak thy Skill.

Orbs proclaim thy Pow'r, Those Motions speak thy Skill.

And on the Wing of ev'ry Hour we read thy Patience still.

And on the Wing of ev'ry Hour we read thy Patience still

And on the Wing of ev'ry Hour we read thy Patience still

D.C. forte

Andante Grazioso

But when we view thy great De _ _ sign

But when we view thy great De _ _ sign

But when we view thy great De _ _ sign

to save re_bellious Worms, Where Vengeance

to save re_bellious Worms, Where Vengeance

to save re_bellious. Worms, Where Vengeance

T. S.

and Com_pas_sion join in their di_vin_est Forms.

and Com_pas_sion join in their di_vin_est Forms.

and Com_pas_sion join in their di_vin_est Forms.

Here the whole _ _ De_ i_ ty is known,

Here the whole _ _ De_ i_ty is known,

Here the whole De_ i_ty is known,

Nor dares a Creature guefs, Which of the Glo_ries bright_eft

Nor dares a Creature guefs, Which of the Glo_ries bright_eft

Nor dares a Creature guefs, Which of the Glo_ries bright_eft

Andante Siciliana.

thone, The Juftice or the Grace. Now the full

thone, The Juftice or the Grace. Now the full

thone, The Juftice or the Grace. Now the full

Glories of the Lamb, A - dorn the heav'nly Plains

Glories of the Lamb, A - dorn the heav'nly Plains

Glories of the Lamb, A - dorn the heav'nly Plains

Bright Seraphs learn Im_man_u_el's Name, and try their choicest

Bright Seraphs learn Im_man_u_el's Name, and try their choicest

Bright Seraphs learn Im_man_u_el's Name, and try their choicest

T. S.

Strains. O, may I bear some humble Part in

Strains. O, may I bear some humble Part in

Strains. O, may I bear some humble Part in

that Im-mor-tal. Song Wonder and Joy shll tune my

that Im-mor-tal Song Wonder and Joy shll tune my

that Im-mor-tal Song Wonder and Joy shll tune my

♮7 ♭7   6   6
4

Heart, and Love command my Tongue.

Heart, and Love command my Tongue.

Heart, a Love command my Tongue.

5   6   6   5
3   4   3

D.C. forte

Cheshunt.

Our Lord is ri_sen from the Dead, Our Je_sus

Our Lord is ri_sen from the Dead, Our Je_sus

is gone up_on high, The Pow'rs of Hell are Captive

is gone up_on high, The Pow'rs of Hell are Cap_tive

led, Dragg'd to the Portals of the Sky. The Pow'rs of

led, Dragg'd to the Portals of the Sky. The Pow'rs of

Hell are cap-tive led, Dragg'd to the Portals of the

Hell are cap-tive led, Dragg'd to the Portals of the

Sky. Dragg'd to the Portals of the Sky. Sy

Sky. Dragg'd to the Portals of the Sky.

Tutti for

There his triump - hal

There his triump - hal

Chariot waits, And An-gels chaunt the so--lemn

Chariot waits, And An-gels chaunt the so--lemn

Lay, Lift up your Heads, ye heav'nly Gates, ye

Lay, Lift up your Heads, ye heav'nly Gates, ye

e - ver - lasting Doors give Way! Lift up your Heads ye

e - ver - lasting Doors give Way! Lift up your Heads ye

heav'nly Gates, ye ye - ver-lasting Doors give Way.

heav'nly Gates, ye e - ver-lasting Doors give Way.

Solo

Loose your Bars of mas-sy Light, And wide un-fold the-

- the--rial Scene; He Gains these Mansions as his Right, re-

-ceive the King of Glo--ry in! He claims these

6 6 6 6   6 6 #   6   4 # 6
                     4   5

Mansions as his Right, re- ceive the King of

9 8   6 5 6   4 3   6   6 6 6 6
          4 # 5

Glo--ry in! re ceive the King Glo--ry in! Sy

6 6 5   6   6   6 6 5
   4 #   5   5   4

Loose your

7 6
4

Bars of mas--sy Light, And wide 'un-fold the-

7   7 6 5   7 5 6   7 5 6
5 4 #   5 3 4   5 3 4

- the - rial Scene, He claims these Mansions as his

Right, re _ _ ceive the King of Glo _ _ ry in! He

claims these Mansions as his Right, re _ _ ceive the

King of Glo _ _ ry in! re _ _ ceive the King of

Glo _ _ ry in!

Tutti for.
Who is the King of Glo_ry. who.
Who is the King of Glo_ry. who.
who. who is the King of Glo_ry who. The Lord that
who. who is the King of Glo_ry who. The Lord that
9 10
all his Foes o'er came, the World, Sin, Death, and Hell o'er
all his Foes o'er came, the World, Sin, Death, and Hell o'er
6 4 7 3 6 4 2 4 6

_threw, And Je_sus, is the Conqu'ror's Name. And Je_sus

_threw, And Je_sus is the Conqu'ror's Name. And Je_sus

is the Conqu'ror's Name. And Je_sus is the Conquror's

is the Conqu'ror's Name. And Je_sus is the Conquror's

Name. Sy

Name.

Lo! his tri-ump-hal Cha-riot waits And An-gels
chaunt the so-lemn Lay Lift up your Heads, ye
heav'nly Gates, Ye e-ver-last-ing Doors give Way.

Lift up your Heads ye heav'nly Gates Ye e-ver-last-ing

Lift up your Heads ye heav'nly Gates Ye e-ver-last-ing

Doors give Way. Who is the King of Glory

Doors give Way. Who is the King of Glory

who. who. who. Who is the King of Glo-ry

who. who. who. Who is the King of Glo-ry

who. The Lord of glo-rious Pow'r pos-sest, The

who. The Lord of glo-rious Pow'r pos-sest, The

King of Saints and An-gels too. God o-ver

King of Saints and An-gels too. God o-ver

all. for e-ver blest. God o-ver all. for

all. for e-ver blest. God o-ver all. for

e _ _ ver blest. God o _ ver all for

e _ _ ver blest. God o _ ver all for

e _ _ ver blest, God o _ ver all for e _ _ ver

e _ _ ver blest. God o _ ver all for e _ _ ver

blest. for e _ _ ver blest.

blest. for e _ _ ver blest.

Somerset

Set by M. M.

Children of the Heav'nly King As ye journey sweetly

Children of the Heav'nly King As ye journey sweetly

sing Sing your SAVIOUR's worthy Praise Glori-ous

sing Sing your SAVIOUR's worthy Praise Glori-ous

in his Works and ways Ye are trav'ling home GOD

in his Works and ways Ye are trav'ling home GOD

In the ways the Fathers trod They are happy now and ye

In the ways the Fathers trod They are happy now and ye

Soon their hap-pi-nefs fhall see Soon their happiness fhall
Soon their hap-pi-nefs fhall see Soon their happiness fhall

see.
see.

3

O, ye banish'd Seed, be glad
CHRIST our Advocate is made,
Us, to save, our Flesh assumes
Brother to our Souls becomes.

4

Shout ye little Flock and blest,
You on JESU'S Throne shall rest,
There your Seat is now prepar'd,
There your Kingdom and Reward.

5

Fear not Brethren, joyful stand
On the Borders of your Land;
JESUS CHRIST, your Father's SON,
Bids you undismay'd go on.

6

LORD obediently we'll go,
Gladly leaving all below;
Only Thou our Leader be,
And we still will follow Thee.

Croydon.

Set by C.L.

'Tis Finish'd 'tis finish'd   Tis Finish'd the Redeemer said,

'Tis finish'd   Tis Finish'd the Redeemer said,

And meekly meekly bow'd   his   dy _ _ _ ing Head,

And meekly meekly   bow'd   his   dy _ _ _ ing Head,

While we this Sentence scan, Whilst   we   this Sentence scan,

While we this Sentence scan, Whilst   we   this Sentence scan,

Largo

Come Sinners and ob--serve the Word Behold the Conquests

Come Sinners and ob--serve the Word Behold the Conquests

of our LORD   Be-hold   the

of our LORD   Be-hold   the

Conquests the Conquests of our   LORD, Compleat for help-less

Conquests the Conquests of our   LORD, Compleat for help-less

Siciliana

Man Compleat for helpless Man. Finish'd the Righteousness of

Man Compleat for helpless Man. Finish'd the Righteousness of

Grace Finish'd for Sinners pard'ning Peace Their mighty Debt is

Grace Finish'd for Sinners pard'ning Peace Their mighty Debt is

paid. Ac-cusing Law cancel'd by Blood, And Wrath of an of-

paid. Ac-cusing Law cancel'd by Blood, And Wrath of an of-

_fended GOD In sweet Oblivion Laid In sweet Oblivion laid.

_fended GOD In sweet Oblivion Laid In sweet Oblivion laid.

(3)

Who now shall urge a second Claim,
The Law no longer can condemn,
  Faith a Release can shew:
Justice itself a Friend appears,
The Prison house a Whisper hears,
  Loose him and let him go.

(4)

O Unbelief injurious Bar
Source of tormenting fruitless Fear,
  Why dost thou yet reply
Where'er thy loud Objection fall,
'Tis finish'd still may answer all,
  And silence ev'ry Cry.

Ipswich

Set by M.M.

Deep in the Dust before thy Throne Our Guilt and our Dis-

Deep in the Dust before thy Throne Our Guilt and our Dis-

-grace we own Great GOD we own th'unhap-py Name whence

-grace we own Great GOD we own th'unhap-py Name whence

sprung our Nature and our Shame, But whilst our Spirits fill'd with Awe, Be-

sprung our Nature and our Shame, But whilst our Spirits fill'd with Awe, Be-

-hold the Terrors of thy Law, We sing the Honours of thy Grace That

-hold the Terrors of thy Law, We sing the Honours of thy Grace That

sent   to   save   a   ruin'd Race, That   sent   to

sent   to   save   a   ruin'd Race, That   sent   to

save   a   ruin'd   Race.   We   sing thine

save   a   ruin'd   Race,   We   sing thine

e..verlasting SON,Who join'd our Nature   to   his   own, A..

e..verlasting SON,Who join'd our Nature   to   his   own, A..

-dam the se - - - cond from the Dust Raises the
-dam the se - - - cond from the Dust Raises the
Ru - -ins of the First. Where Sin did
Ru - -ins of the First. Where Sin did
reign and Death a - - bound, There have the Sons of
reign and Death a - - bound, There have the Sons of

A _ dam found A _ bounding Life There glor_ious

A _ dam found, A_ bounding Life There glor_ious

Grace Reigns through the LORD Our Righteousness. Reigns

Grace Reigns through the LORD Our Righteousness. Reigns

through the LORD Our Righteous _ _ ness

through the LORD Our Righteous _ _ ness

St. Katherine Cree

Sy. Set by C.I.

To GOD the on__ly Wise, Our

To GOD the on__ly Wise, Our

SAVIOUR and our King Let

SAVIOUR and our King Let

all the Saints be__low the Skies Their hum__ble

all the Saints be__low the Skies Their hum__ble

Prais - - es bring Let all the Saints be - -
Prais - - es bring the Saints be - -

- - low the Skies their hum - ble Praises bring.
- - low the Skies their hum - ble Praises bring.

Siciliana Adagio Pia.

'Tis His Almighty Love, His Counsel and his Care, Pre...

...serves us safe from Sin and Death, and ev'ry hurt...full

Snare, Pre...serves us safe from Sin and Death, and

Sy
ev'-ry hurt-full Snare.
ev'-ry hurt-full Snare.
Sy
He will present his Saints. Un-blem--ish'd
He will present his Saints. Un-blem--ish'd
Sy
and com--pleat. Be-fore the Glory of his Face,
and com--pleat. Be-fore the Glory of his

Joys di _ vine _ _ ly great. Be _ fore the Glo _ _ ry

Joys di _ _ vine _ _ ly great, the Glo _ _ ry

of his Face with Joys di _ vine _ ly great.

of his Face with Joys di _ vine _ ly great.

Chorus

Then

all the cho_sen Seed shall meet a_round the
all the cho_sen Seed shall meet a_round the
7 6 6 4 8 6 7
Sy
Throne Shall bless the Conduct of his Grace and
Throne bless the Conduct of his Grace and
make his Wonders known, To our Redeem_ing
make his Wonders known, To our Redeem_ing
♯ 6 4 5 3 4 2 7

God   Wisdom and Pow'r be__longs   Im__

God   Wisdom and Pow'r be__longs   Im__

__mortal Crowns of Ma_jes_ty And e___ver_lasting

__mortal Crowns of Ma_jes_ty And e__ver_lasting

Songs   To   Our Redeeming   God.

Songs   To   Our Redeeming   God.

Wisdom and Pow'r be_longs Im_mortal Crowns of
Wisdom and Pow'r be_longs Im_mortal Crowns of
6 4 5 3
Ma_jes_ty And e_ _ver_lasting Songs Im_
Ma_jes_ty And e_ _ver_lasting Songs Im_
6 4 6 7 6 4 5 3
_ _mortal Crowns of Ma_jes_ty And e_ _ _verlasting Songs
_ _mortal Crowns of Ma_jes_ty And e_ _ _verlasting Songs
6 4 5 3 7 6 5 6 4 5 3 6 4 5 3

260 Litchfield

Set by M.M.
sotto voce dolce

§. Maestoso

To God To God the on-ly wise, Our Saviour
To God To God the on-ly wise, Our Saviour

and our King, Let all the Saints be-low the
and our King, Let all the Saints be-low the

Skies their hum-ble Praises bring. Their hum-ble
Skies their hum-ble Praises bring. Their hum-ble

Praises bring. Let all the Saints below the Skies, Their

Praises bring. Let all the Saints below the Skies, Their

hum-ble Praises bring. The hum-ble Praises bring.

hum-ble Praises bring. The hum-ble Praises bring.

'Tis His Almighty Love, — His Counsel and his Care, Preserves us

'Tis His Almighty Love, — His Counsel and his Care, Preserves us safe from Sin and Death, from Sin and Death, pre__serves us

safe from Sin and Death, from Sin and Death, pre__serves us

safe from Sin and Death,

From Sin and

safe from Sin and Death,

From Sin and

Death, and ev'ry hurtful Snare.

He shall present his Saints Un-

Death, and ev'ry hurtful Snare.

He shall present his Saints Un-

Repeat the 1st Chorus

_blemish'd and com-pleat Be-fore the Glo-ry of his

_blemish'd and com-pleat Be-fore the Glo-ry of his

Face With Joys di-vine---ly great. di---vine--ly

Face With Joys di-vine---ly great. di---vine--ly

great. With Joys------- di-vine--ly great

great. With Joys------- di-vine--ly great

Allegro ma non troppo

Then all the cho_sen Seed Shall meet around his Throne

Then all the cho_sen Seed Shall meet around his Throne

Shall bless the Con_duct of his Grace and makes his

Shall Con_duct of his Grace and makes his

Wonders known and make his Wonders known.

Wonders known and make his Wonders known.

To Our Re_deem_ing God To our Re deeming God

To Our Re_deem_ing God To our Re deeming God

Wisdom and Pow'r Wisdom and Pow'r Wisdom and Pow'r be-longs

Wisdom and Pow'r Wisdom and Pow'r Wisdom and Pow'r be-longs

Im--mortal Crowns of Ma-jes--ty and e--ver-

Unis

Ma-jes--ty and e--ver-

-last-ing Songs and e-ver-last-ing Songs Im-mor-tal

-last-ing Songs and e-ver-last-ing Songs Im-mor-tal

Crowns of Majes--ty and e-ver-last-ing Songs.

Crowns of Majes--ty and e-ver-last-ing Songs.

Exeter. Andante Allegro

Name address. Sy

Name address.

2

God thro' the World extends his Sway,
The Regions of eternal Day
But Shadows of his Glory are,
With Him, whose Majesty excels,
Who made the Heaven in which He dwells,
Let no created Power compare.

3

Tho' his beneath his State they know
In highest Heaven above Angels go,
Yet He to lowlier objects his Care;
He takes the Needy for his Call,
Advancing him in Courts to dwell,
Companion of the greatest there.

4

To Father, Son, and Holy Ghost,
The God whom Heaven's triumphant Host
And suffering Saints on Earth adore.
Be Glory as in Ages past,
As now it is, and so shall last
When Earth and Heaven shall be no more.

Dialogue Hymn

Set by C. B.

Men.

Tell us   Tell us O   Women,   we   would know.

Tell us   Tell us 'O   Women,   we   would know.

Women.

whither so   fast   ye   move,   We, call'd to leave ẏ World be-

whither so   fast   ye   move,   We, call'd to leave ẏ World be-

Men.

_low are seeking are seeking   one   a__bove.   Whence

_low   are   seeking   one   a__bove.   Whence

come ye, Whence came ye say, and what the Place that

come ye, Whence came ye say, what the Place that

Women.

ye are trav'__ling from. From Tri_bu__la_tion,we thro'

ye are trav'__ling·from. From Tri_bu__la_tion,we thro'

Grace, are now are now re__turn__ing Home.

Grace, are now re__turn__ing Home.

(3)
Is not your native Country here?
Like you not this Abode?
We seek a better Country far,
A City built by God.

(4)
Thither we travel, nor intend
Short of that Bliss to rest.
Nor we, till in the Sinner's Friend
Our weary Souls are bless'd.

Chorus. Allgro.

Friends of the Bridegroom we shall reign.

Friends of the Bridegroom we shall reign.

Saviour Saviour we ask no more, we

Saviour Saviour we ask no more, we

ask — — no more. Hail Lamb of God, for

ask — — — no more. Hail Lamb of God, for

Sin _ _ _ners slain,Whom Heav'n and Earth a _ _ do _ re. Whom

Sin _ _ _ners slain,Whom Heav'n and Earth a _ _ do _ re. Whom

Heav'n and Earth a _ do _ _ _ _ _ _ re   Whom

Heav'n and Earth a _ _ _ do _ _ _ _ _ re   Whom

Heav'n   and Earth a _ dore.

Heav'n   and Earth a _ dore.

Amesbury.

Set by S.A.

Come let us a-new our Journey pur-sue, roll round with the

Come let us a-new our Journey pur-sue, roll round with the

Year, roll round with the Year, And never stand still till our

Year, roll round with the Year, And never stand still till our

Master appear, And never stand still till our Master appear.

Master appear, And never stand still till our Master appear.

His a_ _ do_ra_ble Will let us
His a_ _ do_ra_ble Will let us
glad_ly ful_fil, and our Talents im_prove, our Talents im_
glad_ly ful_fil, and our Talents im_prove, our Talents im_
_prove, By the Patience of Hope, and the Labour of Love. By the
_prove, By the Patience of Hope, and the Labour of Love. By the
Tasto Solo

Patience of Hope, and the Labour of Love, the Patience of

Patience of Hope, and the Labour of Love, the Patience of

Hope, and the Labour of Love,

Hope, and the Labour of Love.

Our Life is a Dream, Our Time, as a Stream, glides swiftly a-

Our Life is a Dream, Our Time, as a Stream, glides swiftly away, glides swiftly a_way, and the fu_gi_tive Moment re_

way, glides swiftly a_way, and the fu_gi_tive Moment re_

_fu_ses to stay. The Ar_row is flown. The Moment is

_fu_ses to stay. The Ar_row is flown. The Moment is

gone, the Mil_le_nial Year, Rushes on to our View, and E_

_gone, the Mil_le_nial Year, Rushes on to our View, and E_

276

_ter_ni_ty here. E __ ter_ni_ty's here, the Mil__le_nial

_ter_ni_ty here. E __ ter_ni_ty's here, the Mil__le_nial

Year Rushes   on to our View, and E_ter_ni_ty's here, E_

Year Rushes   on to our View, and E_ter_ni_ty's here, E_

_ter_ni_ty's here, E_ter_ni_ty's here, E__ter_ni_ty's

_ter_ni_ty's here, E_ter_ni_ty's here, E__ter_ni_ty's

Solo Andante

here.

O that each in the Day of his

here.

Coming may say I have fought my Way thro' have fought my Way thro'

I have finish'd the Work Thou didst give me to do. have

finish'd the Work Thou didst give me to do.

Tutti.
O that each from the Lord may re--
O that each from the Lord may re--
--ceive the glad Word, Well and faithful--ly done,
--ceive the glad Word, Well and faithful--ly done,
7
faith-ful-ly done, En-ter in-to my Joy, and sit
faith-ful-ly done, En-ter in-to my Joy, and sit
6 5
6 4
5 3

down on my Throne. Enter in - to my Joy, and sit

down on my Throne. Enter in - to my Joy, and sit

down on my Throne. Enter in - to my Joy, and sit

down on my Throne. Enter in - to my Joy, and sit

down on my Throne. and sit down on my Throne.

down on my Throne. and sit down on my Throne.

Gloria Patri

Set by F. A.

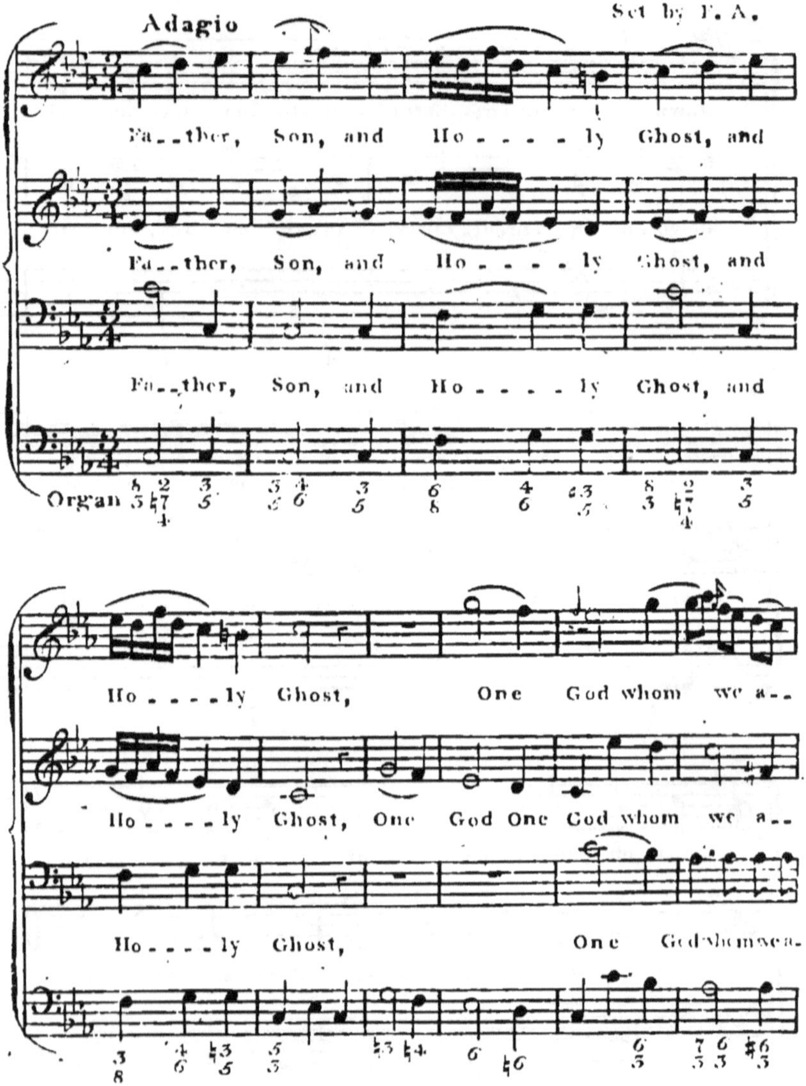

dore. Join we with the heav'n-ly Host

dore. Join we with the heav'n-ly Host

dore. Join we with the heav'n-ly Host

4 #3
5 5   b6   #6   #3   5 6   4 3 4
                                  5

To Praise to praise Thee e-ver-more.

To praise Thee e----ver-more.

To praise praise Thee e----vermore. To

6 5   5 6   #6 6   4 4 6   5 6 5   5 3
                                 4 3 3
                                      3

To praise to praise Thee 'e - - ver more.

To praise ! Thee e - - - - ver more.

praise praise Thee e - - - - ver more.

Live by Heav'n Live by Heav'n and Earth a dor'd.

Live by Heav'n Live by Heav'n and Earth a dor'd.

Live by Heav'n Live by Heav'n and Earth a dor'd.

Three in One, and One in Three. Ho--ly

Three in One, and One in Three. Ho--ly

Three in One, and One in Three. Ho--ly

Ho--ly ho--ly Lord, all Glo-ry be

Ho--ly ho--ly Lord, all Glory be

Ho--ly ho--ly Lord, all Glo----ry

Glo _ ry be to Thee. Three in One and

Glo _ ry be to Thee. Three in One and

Glo _ ry be to Thee. Three in One and

One in Three. Ho _ _ ly Lord. Ho _ _ ly

One in Three. Ho _ _ ly Lord. Ho _ _ ly

One in Three. Ho _ _ ly Lord. Ho _ _ ly

Lord, all Glo_ry all Glo_ry be _ _ _ to

Lord, all Glo_ry all _ Glo_ry be_ _ _ to

Lord, all Glo _ _ _ry all Glo_ry be _ _ _ to

Thee. be_ to Thee. be to Thee.

Thee. be to Thee. be to Thee.

Thee. be to Thee. be to Thee.